Ethical Leadership

Ethical Leadership

*Manuel Mendonca and
Rabindra N. Kanungo*

Open University Press
Maidenhead ● New York

Open University Press
McGraw-Hill Education
McGraw-Hill House
Shoppenhangers Road
Maidenhead
Berkshire
England
SL6 2QL

email: enquiries@openup.co.uk
world wide web: www.openup.co.uk

and Two Penn Plaza, New York, NY 10121–2289, USA

First published 2007

A catalogue record of this book is available from the British Library

ISBN–10: 0335 216 994 (pb) 0335 217 001 (hb)
ISBN–13: 978 0335 216 994 (pb) 978 0335 217 007 (hb)

Library of Congress Cataloguing-in-Publication Data
CIP data applied for

Typeset by YHT Ltd, London
Printed and bound by CPI Group (UK) Ltd, Croydon, CR0 4YY

The *McGraw·Hill* Companies

Dedicated
to those who lead
from moral strength, derived from a free choice of
what is good and true; and not from fear, greed, and
other weaknesses.

Contents

Preface

The need to explore the phenomenon of ethical leadership in organizations is prompted by the increasing societal concern that it is unacceptable for organizational leaders to be indifferent to moral responsibility, much less engage in unethical behaviour. Ethics is to leadership in organizations what the thread is to the spider web hanging from a fence. The thread enables the spider to lower himself and weave his fabric, stretching out to every corner. That thread sustains the whole framework of the web; without it everything loosens. Just as the thread serves the spider to weave the fabric and sustain it, in much the same way, the leader's moral integrity moves and sustains the followers' effort to achieve the common goals of human welfare at personal, organizational, and societal levels.

It is this fundamentally crucial role of the leader that led us ten years ago to examine the behavioural dimensions of ethical leadership. At that time, we found that the issue of ethics in leadership roles was paid scant attention in both the psychological and the management literature on leadership. To address this lack of interest in ethical leadership, we proposed a three-dimensional behavioural framework for the study of the topic in our 1996 book on *Ethical Dimensions of Leadership*. During the past ten years, we have noticed an increasing interest in the study of ethical leadership for better understanding of the phenomenon among behavioural scientists, and management scholars and practitioners. This was clearly evident to us in a McGill University symposium on the topic in 1999 attended by scholars and practitioners belonging to educational, medical, government and business organizations. Following soon after was the first Special Issue of the *Canadian Journal of Administrative Sciences* in December 2001, devoted entirely to ethical leadership and governance in organizations.

This upsurge of interest in the role of ethics in organizational leadership and governance became an impetus for us to revise and update our earlier work (Kanungo & Mendonca, 1996) and write this book. In this book, we have adopted and improved upon the three-dimensional framework of ethical leadership presented in our 1996 book and used materials related to the framework from that book. But the present book goes far beyond this by meeting several deficiencies in our previous work. Specifically, the book critically analyses various theories of moral behaviour or ethics and shows how they can be related to various leadership roles. This brings about an integration of moral and psychological theories of leadership behaviour.

The book not only examines the various modal orientations of leadership, but also demonstrates that true, effective leadership happens when the leader's behaviour and the exercise of leadership influence are consistent with ethical and moral values. Almost no day seems to go by without some media exposure of unethical behaviour of organizational leaders or exhortations about the need for ethics in business and public life. We argue that in ethical leadership, a leader fulfils the obligations that arise from moral principles not from the pragmatic considerations of the impact of bad media exposure on the bottom line or similar organizational interest. Rather, the leader fulfils moral obligations because of virtue, because it conforms to what is good and true.

Second, the book argues that ethical leaders can also be effective leaders. Recent research shows that in order to be effective, leaders must possess a number of critical managerial competencies. In order to be ethical, that is to incorporate moral principles in day-to-day behaviour, leaders need to practise a set of virtues. The book identifies the manifest behaviours in managerial competencies and in leadership virtues, and then goes on to show how ethical leaders can exercise the basic competencies in the pursuit of virtues.

Third, in the book, ethical leadership is viewed as the main spring for the creation of learning organizations in which not only the leaders but followers as well achieve higher levels of personal mastery and efficacy. The book provides compelling arguments for the fact that for ethical leadership the practice of virtues and competencies is indispensable to acquiring personal mastery at all levels within organizations.

Corporate leaders through their actions seem to have created a public perception that profits, regardless of any other consideration, are the major driving force of business and that even unethical means seem to be justified in the relentless pursuit of profit. Business education also seems to be affected by an ethical malaise. As we see from the examples cited in the book, an unusually strong emphasis on self-centredness seems to characterize the values of business students. It is, therefore, not surprising that society demands and expects greater accountability from business organizations and business schools. The leadership of these organizations bears the primary responsibility to respond to these demands. The practice of ethical leadership is indeed the challenge for organizational leaders in the twenty-first century.

The book is intended to serve the needs of business and organizational behaviour related educational programmes, business consultants, and researchers. The use of the book as a primary text or supplemental reading will greatly enhance leadership courses in business schools or executive development programmes. It is also of interest to those on courses in business ethics, organizational behaviour, and managerial skills development. The inclusion of the cultural contingencies in leadership, in the context of non-Western sociocultural environments, extends its suitability and usefulness for courses in international business and international management. The practical orientation, in addition to the conceptual framework, offers practitioners and consultants strategies for effective leadership, such as empowerment, together with suggestions of how leaders can prepare for ethical leadership. Several issues and questions identified in the book are intended to prompt further research and study into the morality of leadership. The questionnaire measures of leadership and managerial competencies included in the appendices may come in handy in future research efforts.

Finally, it is our hope that the book will be sufficiently provocative to arouse and sustain the interest of readers in the issue of how to foster and promote ethical leadership in organizations.

Manuel Mendonça
Rabindra N. Kanungo

1 Need for Ethical Leadership in Organizations

Synopsis

In this introductory chapter we present the context for the discussion of the phenomenon of leadership and its ethical dimensions. For this purpose, we explore some contemporary events and ideas which suggest the absolute and urgent need for moral leadership in organizations and in society if we truly want to achieve the common goal of human welfare at personal, organizational, and societal levels. We then present an overview of the book through a brief summary of the contents of each chapter – thus: a critical review of the theories of ethics; an overview of leadership theory and research; the ethical dimensions of leadership – the leader's motives, influence strategies, and character; preparation for ethical leadership in organizations; cultural contingencies of leadership.

Introduction and overview

> No man is an Island, entire of itself;
> every man is a piece of the Continent, a part of the main;
> if a clod be washed away by the sea, Europe is the less, as well as if a promontory were,
> as well as if a manor of thy friends or of thine own were;
> any man's death diminishes me, because I am involved in Mankind;
> (John Donne, quoted in Bartlett, 1968: 308 b)

Indeed, human beings grow and fulfil themselves through acting and living together with others. The social dimension of human beings creates the necessity for organizations that promote the well-being of their members. The basic feature of these organizations and their constituent elements are people with a set of shared beliefs and values and a common purpose. Through their organization they strive to achieve, consistent with their beliefs and values, the common purpose which they believe is beneficial to them and to the society at large. Organizations serve human beings well. The family, the school, religious institutions – all play a pivotal role in the development of the human being from a helpless infant to an independent, mature, and morally responsible adult. The economic and political institutions contribute to such development through programmes and laws designed to sustain a self-supporting and self-governing society.

The need for leadership in organizations

A closer analysis of organizations would reveal that these are more than a random assembly of people, albeit with a common purpose. Organizations have a structure; organizational members assume or are assigned different tasks, roles, and status levels in the organization in order to achieve this purpose efficiently and effectively. Organizational structures imply that there are leaders and followers. The leaders are expected to provide direction, exercise control, and generally execute such functions that are necessary to achieve the organization's objectives.

In successful organizations, true leadership behaviour – in the sense of leading others – is more than the routine maintenance activities such as allocating resources, monitoring and directing employees, and building the organization's *esprit de corps*. True leadership involves moving followers toward the realization of the vision that the leader has formulated to fulfil the organization's mission. Clearly, organizations need leadership. Without a leader, the organization is much like a rudderless ship, adrift in a turbulent environment. For this reason, the study of leadership, its modal orientations and processes, is an instructive and fruitful endeavour for students of organizations and management practitioners.

The need for ethics in leadership

However, one might legitimately question the need for the study of ethics in leadership. If we think about it, the greatest number of organizations that exist are in the business and government sectors, which, it might be argued, really are or should be unconcerned with ethics or morality. The argument might be that ethics and morality are or ought to be the exclusive preserve of religious and, possibly, educational organizations. When morality intrudes into the business organization, it has the potential of diverting business leaders from the organization's primary objectives and, as a result, causing it to be inefficient and to deprive stockholders of their due returns. Surely, the founder did not start the business to promote morality but rather to earn a profit and create wealth. Similar questions can also be raised about the role of ethics in non-profit organizations, including the government – the largest of all organizations in the country.

The beginnings of a response to these questions can be traced to Aristotle's *Politics*. In this work, Aristotle observed that the state comes into being to provide law and order but continues for the sake of good law, good order, and noble actions. In a similar vein, the *raison d'être* of human organizations – their structure and mechanisms, norms and activity – is to support some 'good' and be in accord with the 'highest excellence'. As Peter Drucker (1968: 461) observed: 'What is most important is that management realize that it must consider the impact of every business policy and business action upon society. It has to consider whether the action is likely to promote the public good, to advance the basic beliefs of our society, to contribute to its stability, strength and harmony'.

All organizational members bear the responsibility to ensure that organizational objectives are achieved in a manner that is consistent with these ideals and serve their own welfare as well as the larger interests of society. However, the primary duty and responsibility for providing the proper direction and the high standards of performance rest chiefly with the organizational leader. Indeed, the leader is the soul of the organization. The leader's vision inspires and articulates the organization's mission; provides the basis for the organization's objectives and goals; communicates the beliefs and values that influence and shape the organization's culture and behavioural norms; and lays the foundation for organizational strategies, policies, and procedures. However, it is the leader's moral principles and integrity that give legitimacy and credibility to the vision and sustain it. When the leader's moral integrity is in doubt, then the leader's vision, however noble, well crafted, and articulated, is viewed with scepticism by the followers, loses its vigour, and is incapable of moving them to work towards its realization.

There is an increasing realization today that business leaders need to become more responsible, not just to their stockholders but also to their other stakeholders – consumers, employees, suppliers, the government, and local communities. Although no one will deny that a business must be profitable, the sole preoccupation with profit to the exclusion or neglect of other considerations is no longer acceptable. Profits – once the be-all and end-all of business – are now viewed as a means to serve the larger interests of society, which, in effect, implies that business decisions should be based on high standards of both economic and ethical performance. A survey of human resource executives found that 67 per cent of the respondents observed that ethics would be more important for organizations in the future (Halcrow, 1987).

Along with the impressive breakthroughs in technology providing new and better products and services, the improved communications transforming the world into a global village, the greater sense of participation in public life, and generally the higher standard of living, we read of the following events and developments in the area of public and private morality that make us question whether the much-hailed economic and social progress in the developed countries is, indeed, 'progress' and, if so, is it worthwhile.

> What several European revolutions, two world wars and numerous depressions could not do to London's Barings Bank in more than 200 years, one 28-year-old employee accomplished with a few computer keystrokes. And the bank collapsed ... management was alerted months ago to the inadequacies of its oversight systems. But management chose to ignore that advice, presumably because everyone seemed to benefit from the system as it was.
>
> (Finlay, 1995: 21)

> Two experimental design studies in the US involving 179 top executives and 203 controllers found that 47 percent of top executives and 41 percent of the controllers made fraudulent decisions that artificially inflated profits to increase their promotion chances.
>
> (Brief, Dukerich, Brown, and Brett, 1996)

> A study of AACSB Business School deans found that deans are more likely to participate in unethical actions if they result in a substantial donation to their school.
>
> (Siguaw, Rockness, Hunt and Howe, 1998)

> A 1966 Harris Poll reported two-thirds of those polled has 'respect for and confidence in our business leaders'; more recently, only one person in five said so. A poll conducted for *Time* reported that 76 per cent of the public saw 'a lack of ethics in business people' as contributing significantly to the decline in moral standards. The *Harvard Business Review*, surveying subscribers, asked: 'In your company, are there business practices you regard as unethical?' Eighty per cent responded with a resounding yes.
>
> (Morgenson, 2004: A–12)

There is an increasing realization today that organizational leaders need to be more sensitive to their moral obligations to the larger society, which includes all their stakeholders such as consumers, employees, suppliers, governments, local communities. It is the recognition of these obligations that has led several large corporations to formulate codes of ethics, set up ethics committees, communication systems for employees to report abuses or seek guidance, ethics training programs, ethics officers, and disciplinary processes (Weaver, Trevino and Cochran, 1999). The code of ethics can be an important reminder that individuals, not the organization, engage in ethical or unethical practices.

However, such ethical codes and structures need to be more than mere 'window dressing'; much less should competitive business advantage become *the* reason for them. A survey of 10,000 randomly selected employees from all levels of six large US corporations that had a formal code of ethics found that 'specific characteristics of the formal ethics or compliance program matter less than broader perceptions of the program's orientation toward values and ethical aspirations. What helps the most are consistency between policies and actions as well as dimensions of the organization's ethical culture such as ethical leadership' (Trevino, Weaver, Gibson, Toffler, 1999: 131). An organization's code of ethics establishes ethical principles that should govern the leader's decisions and behaviours in order that the leader can fulfil the mission of uplifting the moral climate of the organization. Through their principle-centred behaviour, people in leadership positions determine the moral calibre of organizational members, and thereby contribute to the strengthening or the deterioration of the moral fibre of society. This assertion is also confirmed by a study of all of the Fortune 500 Industrial and Fortune 500 Service companies which found that '... much of the guidance for how programs are implemented comes from a firm's top managers and their commitment to ethics' (Weaver, Trevino and Cochran, 1999: 54).

It is, indeed, unfortunate that business organizations have been subjected to so much criticism. We owe a great deal to the business enterprise. It provides us with the products and services we need and with the opportunities to cultivate and make use of our talents, knowledge, and abilities. It also contributes to the economy, and the living standards we enjoy would be unthinkable without the contemporary business organization. The many beneficial and vital breakthroughs in medicine, education, and technology have resulted from the efforts or support of business corporations. And yet the preceding litany of woes has probably provoked the observation that 'our people have lost faith in the basic values of our economic society, and that we need a spiritual rebirth in industrial leadership ... Can it be that our *god of production has feet of clay?* Does industry need a new religion – or at least a better one than it has had?' (Ohmann, 1989: 59). A proper reflection and analysis of this question would suggest that, as an entity, the business corporation is incapable of doing good or evil in society. The most high-profile corporate scandals – Enron Corporation; Martha Stewart Living Omnimedia Inc; Credit Suisse First Boston; Tyco Corporation; WorldCom Inc – suggest that ethical scandals must be directly and entirely attributed to the unethical behaviour of individuals who lead these corporations (Colvin, 2003; Mehta, 2003; Ottawa Citizen, 2004).

There is a growing awareness that ethical principles ought to govern the decisions of our leaders, and that schools ought to regard character formation as the core element of their mission. This would seem to be particularly necessary in the case of management education. Based on a review of theoretical and empirical research, Daboub, Rasheed, Priem and Gray (1995) have developed a model that describes the relationship between the characteristics of the organization's top management team and corporate criminal activity. The model postulates that, other things being equal, the more formal education in management (such as an MBA) that members of top management possess, the higher the chances of corporate criminal activity. The model clearly suggests that management educators do not seem to provide adequate training and formation in business ethics. As Walton (1988) has observed, 'Teachers cannot ignore what leaders cannot do without' (p. 7). Similar sentiments are echoed by Andrews (1989), when he suggests that 'the problem of corporate ethics has three aspects: the development of the executive as a moral person; the influence of the corporation as a moral environment; and the actions needed to map a high road to economic and ethical performance and to mount guardrails to keep corporate wayfarers on track' (p. 99).

It is not enough that managers are intelligent, industrious, and competent in their technical specialty, because studies have shown that, despite these desirable qualities, they might be ineffective 'because they are perceived as arrogant, vindictive, untrustworthy, selfish, emotional, compulsive, over-controlling, insensitive, [and] abrasive' (Hogan, Curphy and Hogan, 1994: 499). In addition to the individual's ethical qualities, the organization's moral environment is equally important. It is most unlikely that the unethical practices cited previously are entirely those of the individual 'rogue' employee. An unethical practice generally involves 'the tacit, if not explicit, cooperation of others and reflects the values, attitudes, beliefs, language, and behavioral patterns that define an organization's operating culture' (Paine, 1994: 106).

The quality of life and the very survival of a human society depend on the moral calibre of its members. However, the moral calibre of members is largely determined by people in leadership positions. The manner in which leaders function in these positions of influence can directly contribute to the strengthening or the deterioration of the moral fibre of society – the lives of Socrates, Buddha, Mohammed, Lao-Tzu, Gandhi, Mother Teresa, to name a few, attest to their salutary influence in their own day, as well as for all time.

The role of a leader has always carried with it grave and onerous responsibilities. In our time, the burden of this role poses rather unique and formidable challenges because of the fundamental shift in societal norms and values. We refer specifically to 'economic imperialism' (Hirsch, 1976; Schwartz, 1986) and the cult of 'self-worship' (Vitz, 1994), which is so pervasive in North America. According to Schwartz (1990), economic imperialism is 'the spread of economic calculations of *interest* to domains that were once regarded as noneconomic' (p. 13). For example, education has come to be viewed by students as an economic investment, and, therefore, students approach it almost entirely based on its potential to generate salary dollars. As a result, the sole criterion to evaluate education is the earning capacity it has bestowed on the students. In the process, the fundamental purpose of and reason for education – that is, the search for truth – is forgotten. Therefore, one should not be surprised at the comment that Harvard Business School graduates seem to think that there is nothing more to life than money, self-interest, fame, and power (Etzioni, 1989). Nor should one be surprised at the findings that 40 per cent to 90 per cent of university students admit to cheating and that it is acceptable so long as one does not get caught (Watson, 1991).

The cult of self-worship is based on the assumption that 'reward for the self (i.e., egoism) is the only functional ethical principle' (Vitz, 1994: xi). Drawing on modern psychological theories of human motivation and personality, whether intended to or not by the theorists, the cult of self-worship or self-theory has spawned a plethora of techniques, programmes, and self-help books designed to make people 'feel good about themselves'. Underlying these approaches is the emphasis on the rights of individuals to self-actualization and fulfilment of their potential in any form or manner they choose without much regard or concern to one's duties and obligations to others. A striking example of this narcissistic self-love is captured in the advice to teachers that they should neither grade their students nor label nor categorize them. Instead, they should make them feel good about themselves (Kramer, 1991). This focus on self is an 'extreme expression of individualistic psychology first created by a frontier society and now supported and corrupted by consumerism. Today it is reinforced by educators who gratify the vanity of even our youngest children with repetitive mantras like: *"The most important person in the whole wide world is you, and you hardly even know you!"'* (Vitz, 1994: 21).

On this issue of self-love, the observation of Donald Campbell (1975), a social psychologist and a former president of the American Psychological Association, is most pertinent:

> There is in psychology today a general background assumption that the human impulses provided by biological evolution are right and optimal, both individually and socially, and that repressive or inhibitory moral traditions are wrong. This assumption may now be regarded as scientifically wrong. Psychology, in propagating this background perspective in its teaching of perhaps 80 or 90 per cent of college undergraduates, and increasing proportions of high school and elementary school pupils, helps to undermine the retention of what may be extremely valuable social-evolutionary systems which we do not fully understand. (pp. 1120–1)

The preceding sampling of contemporary events and ideas suggests there is an absolute and urgent need for moral leadership in organizations, and in society if we truly want to achieve the common goal of human welfare at personal, organizational, and societal levels. It is in the context of such need that we discuss the phenomenon of leadership and its ethical dimensions because, for better or for worse, organizational leaders are ultimately and unquestionably the fundamental agents of change.

An overview of the book

We first begin with a critical review of the theories of ethics (Chapter 2). After a brief exploration of the classical philosophy of ethics, the chapter explores the sources of moral standards that are inherent – implicitly or explicitly – in various ethical theories, more specifically, the consequentialist and non-consequentialist theories; absolutists and relativists. The chapter then explores personalism – an integrated theory derived from an examination of the nature of the human condition and experience – that is, human beings seeking to live and grow as persons in a world with many other persons. The principles of morality that flow from personalism serve as a solid foundation for the moral life – in particular, for altruism as a principle of moral behaviour. The discussion of altruism, its characteristics and manifest behaviours, provides the basis to assess the nature of ethical leadership in Chapter 4 – more specifically, the ethics of the leader's motives, influence strategies, and character.

Chapter 3 is a brief overview of leadership theory and research. We will explore the diversity of approaches and empirical findings that have led some to observe that there is a crisis in leadership research. In an effort to address this issue of the lack of a unifying comprehensive theoretical framework, the chapter identifies the modal orientations of leadership theory and research on essentially three aspects: leader role behaviour, contingencies of leadership effectiveness, and the leader-follower influence process. It then assesses the limitations of existing theoretical paradigms and examines the emerging trends in leadership theory and research – in particular, the neo-charismatic paradigm. The chapter concludes with an exploration of representative formulation of the neo-charismatic paradigm – a model of charismatic or transformational leadership, which we believe best responds to the needs of organizations in a highly turbulent environment and in the context of increasing globalization of business and interdependence among nations. The discussion describes the model – the behavioural components, the influence process, the attribution of charisma, and the outcomes of charismatic leadership behaviours.

The ethical dimensions of leadership – the leader's motives, influence strategies, and character – are discussed in Chapter 4 in the light of altruism as the principle of moral behaviour, referring to Chapter 2. The overarching motive for ethical leadership is the leader's altruistic intent as opposed to egotistic intent. Although leaders' behaviours are motivated by needs such as affiliation, achievement, and power, these behaviours are effective only to the degree that the nature and manner of such motivation becomes an operative manifestation or expression of altruism. The two basic influence strategies – transactional and transformational – are discussed. It is seen that, unlike the transactional influence strategy, the transformational influence process enhances the follower's self-growth, their self-worth, and enables them to function as an autonomous person. Consequently, when leaders use the transformational influence process, their leadership is more likely to be effective. Finally, the chapter concludes with a discussion of the need for the leader's moral character formation, which enables the leader to prepare themselves and their organizations to meet the challenging demands of the ethical imperative. The leader's moral character formation is discussed at great length in Chapter 5.

The thrust of the preceding chapters is to develop the idea that the expertise and experience, styles and impression management, and other techniques and accoutrements of a leader are effective only to the extent that these are imbued with sound ethical principles. Therefore, in Chapter 5, the focus is on what leaders can do to prepare themselves to function as ethical leaders. It begins with a discussion of the reasons why altruism is needed in organizations and some obstacles to its expression. In business management, the objective of the study of ethics has traditionally been the development of analytical and decision-making skills through exercises in resolving ethical dilemmas and quandaries. Such an approach to the study of ethics might be seen by the students as a purely intellectual exercise rather than as a means to the development of moral insights and the formation of character through the practice of human and moral virtues. As a result, ethics has been treated as distinct and separate from spirituality. The discussion in the chapter demonstrates that spirituality is an integral part of ethics. It provides sustenance to the leader's efforts to develop a moral character possessed of inner strength and resourcefulness, and to create a moral environment in the organization. It also explores some of the sources that spiritual sages of all time recommend that leaders draw on for the needed spiritual strength, solace, and inspiration to exercise the leadership that is uplifting to themselves and their followers.

Chapter 6, the concluding chapter, discusses how cultural variables influence leadership effectiveness in relation to the exercise of the leader role behaviours and the leadership influence process. In the chapter, we first propose a conceptual framework that identifies the major cultural dimensions that might facilitate or hinder leadership effectiveness in non-Western cultures, and discuss a leadership mode that is more appropriate in the context of non-Western cultures. The chapter then explores the question of whether the cultural norms and values that prevail in non-Western societies are compatible with the moral values that are inherent in the altruistic ethic. This discussion demonstrates that although the major religions that have shaped the cultural norms and values of non-Western societies might have different and even contradictory theological insights and responses to this question, there is remarkable consensus on the ethics of human behaviour; it would seem as if the norms of moral behaviour are deeply ingrained in human nature.

Suggested questions for reflection

- Why do organizations need leaders?
- Why do leaders in organizations not pay attention to ethical issues?
- Do ethics have a place in business?
- What can ethical leadership do for our organizations and for society at large?

2 Theories of ethics: a critical review

Synopsis

In the context of the need for moral leadership in organizations and in society, established in the previous chapter, it is imperative that we search for the true moral principles to rely on when making moral judgements. For this reason, the chapter focuses on a critical review of the theories of ethics: the classical philosophy of ethics; the teleological and deontological approaches to ethics; and personalism. Our review of these theories suggests that the principles of morality that flow from personalism serve as a solid foundation for the moral life – in particular, for altruism as a principle of moral behaviour. The chapter concludes with a discussion of altruism – its characteristics and manifest behaviours, which provide the basis to assess, in subsequent chapters, the nature of ethical leadership – more specifically, the ethics of the leader's motives, influence strategies, and character.

Introduction

Ethical acts are based on moral principles that are universal because they incorporate fundamental values such as truth, goodness, beauty, courage, and justice. These values are found in all cultures, although cultures may differ with regard to the application of these values. This chapter critically reviews the ethical theories which are the sources of the differences in the application of these universal values. Thomas Aquinas once observed 'Philosophy is not studied in order to find out what people may have thought but in order to discover what is true'. Following this observation, the underlying approach of this review is the search for the true moral principles to rely on when making moral judgements – distinguishing right actions from wrong actions.

After a brief exploration of the classical philosophy of ethics, the chapter explores the sources of moral standards that are inherent – implicitly or explicitly – in various ethical theories, more specifically, the consequentialist and non-consequentialist theories; absolutists and relativists. The chapter then explores personalism – an integrated theory derived from an examination of the nature of the human condition and experience – that is, human beings seeking to live and grow as persons in a world with many other persons. The principles of morality that flow from personalism will serve, in later chapters, as the basis to assess the nature of ethical leadership.

The nature of morality

What specifically do we understand and mean by 'ethics'? The Concise Oxford Dictionary defines 'ethics' as: '... relating to morals ... treating of moral questions ... rules of conduct ... the whole field of moral science' (1964, p.415). When we explore further the meaning of 'moral', we find it defined as: '... concerned with character or disposition or with the distinction between right and wrong' (p. 784).

According to Solomon (1984), the etymology of ethics suggests its basic concerns; (1) individual character, including what it means to be a good person; and (2) the social rules that govern and limit our conduct, especially the ultimate rules concerning right and wrong, which we call morality. Ethical theories, in general, provide guidelines for making moral decisions by articulating the moral standards which are the basis for moral behaviour.

One characteristic of moral standards that distinguishes them from other standards is that moral standards concern behaviour that can be of serious consequence to human beings and human welfare (Velasquez, 1982). The moral norms against lying, stealing, and murder relate to actions that can harm people; and the moral principle that requires human beings to be treated with respect enhances the dignity of the human being. The soundness of moral standards depends on the adequacy of the reasons that support or justify these standards (Shaw and Barry, 1989). Morals or ethics go well beyond etiquette, protocol and even the mere observance of the laws of the country. It is not a question of an act being legal or illegal, but whether the act is good or evil. A legal act may not necessarily be a morally good act. For example, at the Nuremberg trials all the accused had committed acts that were perfectly 'legal' but not morally good.

Theories of ethics

Classical philosophy of ethics

The ethical views that constitute the major tradition of Western thought can be traced to the philosophical schools in ancient Greece and Rome – notably, the work of Aristotle (384–322 BC) – and developed further in the Middle

Ages, in particular by Thomas Aquinas. According to this tradition, the purpose of human existence is happiness, and this is reached by observing the natural law, a set of basic moral principles and norms that correspond to human nature and can be known by the use of reason. In this tradition, the moral law is synonymous with the natural law. As Thomas Aquinas observed: '... the good of man is to be in accordance with reason, and evil is to be against reason' (Mothershead, 1955: 288). Right and wrong are not just matters of human opinion or inclination but are grounded in the nature of things.

According to Thomas Aquinas, a morally good act has three parts or factors: (1) the objective act itself; (2) the subjective motive of the actor; and (3) the situation or circumstances in which the act is done (Kreeft, 1990). Thus, to act justly is an objectively good act, just as to murder is an objectively evil act. The actor must always have good intentions. For example, making charitable donations only to avoid paying income tax vitiates the moral goodness of an objectively good act. The situation or circumstances must also be considered. Thus, giving alms to the poor is, other things being equal, a morally good act; but refusing alms to the poor person who you know would seriously endanger his or her health by spending it on an alcoholic or drug addiction, is equally a morally good act. Hence, if an act is to be morally good it must be right in respect of all the three parts.

This three-part structure of a moral act provides a sound framework for assessing moral actions and systems. Thus, in assessing the morality of an act one cannot focus only on the objective moral law and ignore the individual's motive and related circumstances. If we do, then the act of killing, even though that was the only way of defending oneself, would be an immoral act. Theories or theorists that take such a position might be said to engage in 'unthinking legalism'. The ethical system of moral subjectivism concentrates on only the second factor – that is, the subjective motive. Thus, a moral subjectivist defends his actions entirely in terms of his or her own motive and pays no attention to the nature or characteristics of the objective act, and the circumstances of the situation. An example of moral subjectivism would be the views expressed in a newsletter of a Mensa chapter in Los Angeles: 'Those people who are so mentally defective that they cannot live in society should, as soon as they are identified, be humanely dispatched' (Mensa Chapter, 1995, p. A.6).

The third popular ethical system today is 'situation ethics'. This system focuses only on the situation, or the situation and the motive – as is the case when one argues that the end justifies the means. The recent public discussion of the morality of the atomic bombing of Hiroshima and Nagasaki to end the third world war underscores this point. Even the 'just war' theory does not provide a justification for an indiscriminate use of means to achieve an end. The intended and unintended consequences of the means that are used ought to be examined – that is, the objective nature of the acts that are involved. If we do not then we deny that we should also consider the first factor which makes an act moral – that is, the objective nature of the act (Kreeft, 1990).

Although the classical philosophy of ethics provides a solid base for the development of sound moral principles, this approach does not specifically consider human experience, as it relates to such principles.

Normative theories of ethics

Moral principles provide a conceptual framework to guide the making of moral decisions; to distinguish right actions from wrong actions. But there is no consensus on what these principles are; instead, we have a variety of different moral principles and ethical considerations. These can be categorized into *consequentialist* (utilitarian) and *non-consequentialist* (Kantian) theories which have been dominant throughout much of the twentieth century.

Consequentialist theories

The consequentialist theories, also known as the 'teleological' approach to ethics, argue that the moral rightness of an action is determined solely by its outcomes or results, and not by the intent of the individual. Thus, if the act's consequence is good, then the act is right; if the consequence is bad, then the act is wrong. The two most important consequentialist theories are: *egoistic hedonism and utilitarianism.*

Egoistic hedonism

To an egoistic hedonist, an act is moral when it promotes the individual's best long-term interests. An egoistic hedonist may seek pleasure or make sacrifices, act honestly or dishonestly or be helpful to others – each of these actions is considered to be moral only if it eventually serves the egoist's best interests. In egoistic hedonism there is no moral duty to act in the interests of others – unless it is the only way to promote one's own self-interest. There seems to be an implicit belief that seeking and finding your own private happiness will inevitably lead to the benefit of everyone else. The rationale for egoistic hedonism is the belief that it is the nature of human beings to be 'selfish'; hence, it is just not possible for human beings to engage in unselfish actions. The thinking underlying egoistic hedonism can be traced to ancient Greece – to the Cyrenaics and Epicureans (Mothershead Jr, 1955).

There are serious questions with regard to the validity of egoistic hedonism as a sound moral principle. First, one expects that moral principles apply equally to the conduct of all persons; and that one is objective and impartial in their application. Egoistic hedonists are not objective, as they are only influenced by their own best interests. Second, they ignore the objective act itself and, as a result, an act such as stealing and murder can be regarded as perfectly ethical so long as it satisfies the actor's long-term self-interest. Such a moral principle is inconsistent with the basic notion of justice.

Utilitarianism

Founded on the principle of utility of David Hume, the major proponents of the utilitarian movement were Jeremy Bentham and John Stuart Mill. In essence, this moral doctrine prescribes that we should always act so as to produce the greatest possible balance of good, pleasure, or comfort, over bad, pain, or discomfort, for everyone affected by our action. Thus, according to utilitarianism, the primary rule of human morality is the maximization of pleasure for the greatest possible number of people with a minimum of discomfort for the same number.

The feasibility of using the theory is questionable because of the difficulty in assessing the likely results of alternative courses of action and in computing the quantum and degree of the 'good'. Even if these aspects are feasible, it is questionable if people will, in fact, take the time needed to do these calculations – accurately and objectively. The theory implicitly accepts that the 'end justifies the means'. By this theory, it is morally acceptable to produce the end (consequences or results) by any means (act) regardless of how abhorrent the act might be. Hence, no act is inherently objectionable; rather, it is objectionable only when it leads to a lesser amount of 'good' than that which could have been produced. Utilitarianism, in reality, involves two principles: greatest good, greatest number. It is not uncommon to be in a situation in which an act can produce the greatest good, but may not produce it for the greatest number; and vice versa. Utilitarianism does not provide a means of determining which act is the morally right act.

As discussed at some length in Chapter 5, hedonistic psychology and utilitarian moral philosophy can result in egotistical behaviour at the organizational level and produce many social 'evils' rather than social 'goods'.

Non-consequentialist theories

Non-consequentialist theories, also known as deontological theories, unlike utilitarianism, are not concerned with consequences but with the duties or obligations of an individual. Thus, actions have true moral worth only when they spring from the recognition of duty and with the intention of discharging that duty. Immanuel Kant is one of the foremost proponents of this approach.

Kant's categorical imperative

Moral rules can, in principle, be known by reason itself. As a rational being, I have an obligation to act. This obligation leads me to ask 'what is the morally right act?' Kant's categorical imperative states that: *my act is morally right in a given situation if and only if I am willing that every person could act in the same way for the same reason.* The underlying logic or major test of a morally right act is whether its principle can be applied to all rational beings, and applied consistently. The test is not whether people in fact accept it; but whether all rational beings, thinking rationally, would accept it, regardless of whether they are the doers or the receivers of the actions. Kant's idealism is a useful method of moral reasoning. Contrary to utilitarianism, it prescribes that the end does not justify the means. Hence, we cannot treat a person as means to an end; to treat a person simply as means would be to view the person as a 'thing' and, thereby, fail to recognize the dignity of the human person.

In the discussion of 'personalism' – refer to the next section – we see that the true foundation of ethical life is in the experience of being the efficient cause of one's own actions based on freedom and truth. Although both the intellect and the will are involved in the act of the human person, the efficient causality of the person consists in the will which, as confirmed by contemporary psychology of the will, has two aspects. One aspect is the will's *actual dynamic element*, which is the free spontaneous movement of the will towards any kind of good. The other aspect is the will's *motive* for the choice of a specific good. The intellect presents to the will the truth of the value of a good (motive) and thereby the will moves spontaneously (actual dynamic element) towards a specific good. Kant constructs his ethics on the categorical imperative, which is the *a priori* form of practical reason. In doing so, he emphasizes the motive, which is one aspect of the will. However, he places less emphasis on the *a posteriori* data of human experience; and, as a result, the dynamic character of the will is not emphasized.

Another limitation of Kant's idealism is that the act is moral only if the person is motivated by the desire to conform to the law. If the person's compliance with the moral law is motivated by the pressure of hedonistic pleasure, or by sheer habit, then such compliance would not have moral value. For Kant, reverence for the duty, implicit in the categorical imperative, is the only emotion that is morally valuable (Kupczak, 2000).

Personalism
Personalism is an affirmation of the absolute value of the human person. Our focus is on the personalist philosophy of Karol Wojtyla, an existential personalism that is metaphysically explained and phenomenologically described (Schmiesing, 2004). Aristotle and Thomas Aquinas had built their philosophies from the foundation of cosmology – a general theory of the universe, an ordered system of ideas. But moving to a theory of the human person from a general theory of the universe did not leave much room for an analysis of human experience.

In addition, with the philosophical approaches of the empiricists and idealists, philosophy did not have much to say about our everyday life experiences. The empiricists reduced human experience to things such as sensory data, neural reactions, and chemical compositions; whereas the idealists seeking to explain everything in terms of ideal types and categories operated in a world of extreme abstraction and subjectivism. In response to this way of doing philosophy, Edmund Husserl founded the new philosophical method of 'phenomenology' – an approach to philosophy which re-links philosophical reflection to objective reality. Unlike the empiricists and the idealists, the phenomenologist focused on the human experience as a whole – its psychological, physical, moral, and conceptual elements – in order to understand what it tells us about the human condition (Novak, 1997).

Wojtyla drew on phenomenology – in particular, Max Scheler's phenomenology of the ethics of value – to create a solid philosophical foundation for the moral life. In effect, he synthesized the two approaches to doing philosophy: the metaphysical realism of Aristotle and Thomas Aquinas, and the sensitivity to human experience and human subjectivity of Max Scheler's phenomenology, which he grounded in a realistic theory of the capacity of human beings to get at the truth of things (Kupczak, 2000). Through this synthesis, we can think through the relationship between the objective truth of things-as-they-are and our subjective or personal experience of that truth. This way of philosophical thinking provides two profound insights on the nature and uniqueness of the human person, and serves as a sound foundation of ethics.

First, it enables us to understand ourselves as 'persons'. As we reflect on the nature of human experience, we find that it can, in essence, be reduced to the experience of: (a) 'things that happen to me'; and (b) 'things I make happen'. In the former experience, I am the object of the action – in effect, I am 'something'. In the latter experience, I think through a decision and then I freely act on it. I am the subject, the efficient cause of my action; in effect, I am 'somebody' – that is, a person. Wojtyla's personalist philosophy incorporates the contemporary psychology of the will, which defines it as '. . . a specific experience in which the personal "I" experiences himself as an efficient cause' (Kupczak, 2000: 34). Narziss Ach and other representatives of *Gestaltpsychologie* broke with the typical nineteenth-century psychological conviction that the will does not form a distinct psychic element and should be reduced to an emotion or a sensation. Instead, they maintained that the human experience reveals the 'actual moment of the will', which manifests itself as 'I really want'; and described the entire activity of the will from the appearance of a motive to the moment of decision (Kupczak, 2000).

Second, it shows 'moral action' as the experience of the transcendence of the human person by a truly human act – one in which the person's decision is free and consistent with the truth. 'The moral values of honesty and courage, through honest and courageous action, become an honest and courageous person' (Schmitz, 1993: 49). For example, I choose to pay a debt that I have freely contracted rather than to cheat on my debt. If the motive for my act is the fear of jail or guilt feelings, then my act is merely a response to external conditions or internal pressures; and, therefore, it is not a truly human act. If the choice to pay the debt is not forced upon me, and I pay the debt because reason tells me that it is good and right to do so, then my act is a truly human act – a free choice of what is good and true. In acting freely and in conformity with the truth, I experience myself as the efficient cause of my actions and grow as a *person* – from the person-I-am to the person-I-ought-to-be (Weigel, 2001).

From the foregoing discussion, it can be seen that the person and his/her action constitute a single, deeply cohesive reality. In performing an action, the person fulfils himself/herself – that is, realizes his/her potential as a person. However, the person's fulfilment is accomplished not by the mere performance of an action but by the positive moral value of the action. Contrary to the empiricists and idealists, Wojtyla's personalist philosophy demonstrates ... 'how moral action, not the psyche or the body, is where we find the center of the human person, the core of our humanity. For it is in moral action that the mind, the spirit and the body come into the unity of a person' (Weigel, 2001: 176).

Hence, morally good actions bring fulfilment and morally evil actions bring non-fulfilment. Inherent to the rational nature of the human being is the obligation of every person to assess the subject matter which the intellect presents to the will for a decision, and make a decision that conforms to the truth. As one strives to fulfil this obligation, one develops one's 'conscience, or *synedesis*, as medieval writers called it ... a disposition to apprehend what is right in particular' (Mothershead, Jr, 1955: 295). From the fulfilment of this obligation emerges the right of a person to follow his or her conscience, which can be regarded as the entire effort of the person to grasp the truth in the domain of moral values. However, the freedom of conscience is always and only freedom in the truth. The essential link between freedom and truth clearly stipulates the proper exercise of freedom; it is not the freedom to do what I feel like doing, but the freedom to do what I ought to do. The conscience indicates the moral values of particular actions, and guides the person with regard to his or her moral duty to do or to avoid doing something (Kupczak, 2000).

A person fulfils himself/herself through free and responsible actions. But, a person also has a social nature and lives in a world with many other persons. This fact necessitates that the person acts together with others in such a way that the person can fulfil himself or herself through participation with others. Participation with others can take two forms – one is 'individualism'; the other is 'objective totalism'. 'Individualism sees in the individual the supreme and fundamental good, to which all the interests of the community or the society have to be subordinated, while objective totalism relies on the opposite principle and unconditionally subordinates the individual to the community or the society' (Wojtyla, 1979: 273). Individualism is inadequate because it limits participation. The 'others' are perceived as an obstacle to the growth of the person when, in fact, interaction with others is a vital source of the growth and development of the person. Under individualism, the community would be manipulated to primarily protect and serve the interests of the individual from 'others'. The effects of individualism – a strong emphasis on individual accomplishment and material prosperity, even at the expense of others – are discussed in Chapter 5. Totalism is also inadequate because it assumes that the common good can only be attained by severe limitations on the freedom of the individual – even to the extent of using coercion. Totalism strips the person of freedom and, as a consequence, the person is denied fulfilment in acting and living together with others.

Clearly, the person's participation – that is, acting-together-with-others – ought to serve both the individual and the common good. What attitude will foster such participation and nurture a truly human society? Wojtyla (1979) analyses four 'attitudes': conformism; non-involvement; opposition or resistance; solidarity. Two of these attitudes, conformism and non-involvement, serve neither the individual nor the community. Conformism denotes a tendency to comply with the accepted practices and to assimilate with the community, which could be a sign of solidarity with the community. However, it could also be an acceptance of community standards and practices based not on conviction or free choice but solely for the purpose of acquiring some benefit to self. Such a servile attitude of conformism does harm both to the person and the community. The attitude of non-involvement reflects a lack of concern for the common good. In some situations, individuals may find that solidarity with the community is difficult, and that expressing opposition is not justified. In these situations, non-involvement may be a form of communicating a message. Nevertheless, participation is a fundamental good of a community; the attitude of non-involvement would prevent persons from fulfilling themselves in acting 'together with others'.

The other two attitudes – opposition and solidarity – serve both the individual and the common good. Opposition is an authentic attitude when out of a deep concern for the common good, one resists the injustice that exists. In such a situation, those who oppose do not cut themselves off from their community. Rather, they engage in a dialogue in order to bring to light what is right and true and develop a constructive resolution of the differences. The dialogue that is involved in these situations, however serious the conflicts might be, contributes to the development of the person and greatly enriches the community.

Solidarity is, indeed, the primary authentic attitude toward society.

> The attitude of solidarity is, so to speak, the natural consequence of the fact that human beings live and act together; it is the attitude of a community, in which the common good properly conditions and

initiates participation, and participation in turn properly serves the common good, fosters it, and furthers its realization. 'Solidarity' means a constant readiness to accept and to realize one's share in the community because of one's membership within that particular community. In accepting the attitude of solidarity man does what he is supposed to do not only because of his membership in the group, but because he has the 'benefit of the whole' in view: he does it for the 'common good.' The awareness of the common good makes him look beyond his own share; and this intentional reference allows him to realize essentially his own share. Indeed, to some extent, solidarity prevents trespass upon other people's obligations and duties, and seizing things belonging to others ... It is this attitude that allows man to find the fulfillment of himself in complementing others.

(Wojtyla, 1979: 284–5)

The reality of the person existing and acting 'together with others' extends to being a fellow member of a community as well as a neighbour.

The notion of 'neighbour' is strictly related to man as such and to the value itself of the person regardless of any of his relations to one or another community or to the society. The notion takes into account man's humanness alone – that humanness which is the possession of every man just as much as it is my own. It thus provides the broadest basis for the community a basis that extends beyond any strangeness or foreignness, as well as beyond the strangeness that results from membership in different human communities.

(Wojtyla, 1979: 349–50)

By its affirmation of the absolute value of the human person, the personalistic principle requires that the person cannot be treated as an object of use – as the means to an end; and that the only proper and adequate attitude towards the person is love.

The person is a being for whom the only suitable dimension is love. We are just to a person if we love him. ... love is not limited to excluding all behavior that reduces the person to a mere object of pleasure. It requires more; it requires the affirmation of the person as a person ... and the sincere gift of self ... Man affirms himself most completely by giving of himself.

(John-Paul II, 1994: 201–2)

The personalist philosophy is indeed a solid foundation for the moral life – in particular, for altruism as a principle of moral behaviour. Altruism is highly regarded in all cultures as the epitome of sound moral principles. The commandment to love one's neighbour is universal to all religious traditions, as we can see from the following quotations: (cited in Shaw & Barry, 1989)

> Good people proceed while considering that what is best for others is best for themselves.
>
> (*Hitopadesa*, Hinduism)

> Thou shalt love thy neighbour as thyself.
>
> (*Leviticus 19:18*, Judaism)

> Therefore all things whatsoever ye would that men should do to you, do ye even so to them.
>
> (*Matthew 7:12*, Christianity)

> Hurt not others with that which pains yourself.
>
> (*Udanavarga 5:18*, Buddhism)

> What you do not want done to yourself, do not do to others.
>
> (*Analects 15:23*, Confucianism)

> No one of you is a believer until he loves for his brother what he loves for himself.
>
> (*Traditions*, Islam)

Even those whose behaviour is inconsistent with this moral principle rarely deny its validity. On the contrary, they might argue that circumstances or conditions prevent them from acting altruistically. Therefore, we can develop the ethical dimensions of leadership based on altruism as a fundamental principle of moral behaviour. For this purpose, the sections that follow will explore the following questions: What is the nature and characteristics of altruism? What are its manifest behaviours?

Altruism – its characteristics and manifest behaviours

> A certain man went down from Jerusalem to Jericho, and fell among thieves, which stripped him of his raiment, and wounded him, and departed, leaving him half dead. And by chance there came down a certain priest that way: and when he saw him, he passed by on the other side. And likewise a Levite, when he was at the place, came and looked on him, and passed by on the other side. But a certain Samaritan, as he journeyed, came where he was: and when he saw

him, he had compassion on him. And went to him, and bound up his wounds, pouring in oil and wine, and set him on his own beast, and brought him to an inn, and took care of him. And on the morrow when he departed, he took out two pence, and gave them to the host, and said unto him. Take care of him; and whatsoever thou spendest more, when I come again, I will repay thee.

(Luke 10: 30–35)

This biblical story captures the essence of altruistic behaviour. We see in this story three types of behaviour. First, the behaviour of the thieves, who deliberately harmed the traveller for their personal gain. Second, the priest and the Levite, who demonstrated complete apathy to avoid the personal costs or inconvenience from being involved. Third, the Samaritan, who went through considerable self-sacrifice to help the traveller. Clearly the Samaritan's behaviour is commonly seen as altruistic, whereas the other two types of behaviour are perceived as egotistical. The Samaritan is seen as being motivated by a concern for the benefit of others and a disregard for his own personal costs. On the other hand, the behaviour of the thieves, the priest, and the Levite is perceived as motivated by a concern for benefits and costs to themselves and by a disregard for the benefits and costs to others. Of course, as will be discussed later, a clear moral difference exists between the behaviour of the thieves and that of the priest and Levite. But these are grouped together because their behaviour can be categorized as 'benefiting self'. It is the criteria of 'benefiting others' versus 'benefiting self' that distinguishes altruistic behaviours from egotistical behaviours.

What is altruism?

Social psychologists define altruism in two ways. First, as an attributed dispositional intent to help others – as a 'Willingness to sacrifice one's welfare for the sake of another' (Krebs, 1982: 55); as behaviour intended to benefit others without the expectation of an external reward (Macaulay and Berkowitz, 1970). Second, in terms of the manifest behaviour and its consequences without any reference to one's dispositional intentions. Thus, altruism is that behaviour '. . . that renders help to another person' (Worchel, Cooper, and Goethals, 1988: 394) regardless of the intention of the help-provider. The first type of definition can be said to refer to altruism as internal state; the second type refers to it as behaviour with consequences. Since it is often difficult to identify the help-provider's dispositional intentions, researchers have preferred to define altruism as a form of overt behaviour that benefits others. As a behavioural construct, altruism has a much broader scope which covers both intentions and actions. The actions take many forms of prosocial behaviour, such as charity, helping, cooperation, empowering, and so on. These behaviours benefit others regardless of whether these are intended to be selfless or otherwise. As a behavioural construct, one can also explore the underlying motivational processes that energize, direct, and maintain altruistic intentions and behaviours in individuals.

What are the reasons for altruistic behaviour?

The existing motivational theories confirm and support our intuitive understanding that all human acts seek to achieve some purpose or goal. Altruistic acts also share this basic characteristic. Although altruistic acts are directed primarily for the express purpose of benefiting others, these acts also satisfy some needs of the individual. This latter characteristic has given rise to the 'hedonistic paradox', which questions the existence of altruism. The question is posed thus: if an act that benefits others also benefits the actor, then how can it be termed as 'altruistic'? In dealing with this question, we need to recognize a common assumption held by psychologists that all behaviour – whether directed towards benefiting oneself or another – is energized by some needs or inner drives without which human behaviour would simply not occur. It is, therefore, to be expected that altruistic behaviours must necessarily stem from an inner need state. These behaviours are directed primarily to fulfil the individual's objective or intention of benefiting others. In the process of meeting this objective, the behaviours do satisfy some needs of the individual, but the existence in human beings of the deeper-level need for altruism, which is the source of these behaviours, cannot be denied. For this reason, the 'hedonistic paradox' that questions the existence of altruism is much like the chicken-and-egg conundrum: it is a non-issue.

Altruistic behaviour defined as benefiting others can stem from internal need states, such as a 'nurturance' need, postulated by Murray (1938) and later by Jackson (1967). Psychologists generally view nurturance as a learned psychological need; and sociobiologists argue that genetic pre-programming underlies the altruistic behaviour mechanism (Wilson, 1978). It is rather difficult to determine the validity of a genetic basis for altruism. For this reason, we shall examine the two major explanations offered by social psychologists which help us understand how human beings acquire the need for nurturance or altruism. The two explanations are anchored in the notions of the reciprocity norm and the social responsibility norm. Through the socialization process, we develop these internal norms, which operate as a motivational force and guide our behaviour.

Human beings develop an internal moral code of reciprocity that dictates that individuals will help those who have helped them (Gouldner, 1960). This norm generally applies when people are interacting with their equals or with those who possess greater resources. However, when individuals deal with their dependants who are unable to reciprocate, then the inner moral code of social responsibility may be evoked. The norm of social responsibility refers to an internalized belief that to help others without any consideration, such as an expected future personal benefit, in return, is a moral imperative (Berkowitz, 1972; Schwartz, 1975). Such internalized beliefs regarding social and moral obligations constitute the basis of an altruistic motive that, in turn, energizes altruistic behaviour.

The manifest behaviours of altruism

The different forms of altruistic behaviours can be identified and distinguished from the different forms of egotistical behaviour in terms of the polar dimensions presented in Figure 2.1 (Kanungo and Conger, 1993).

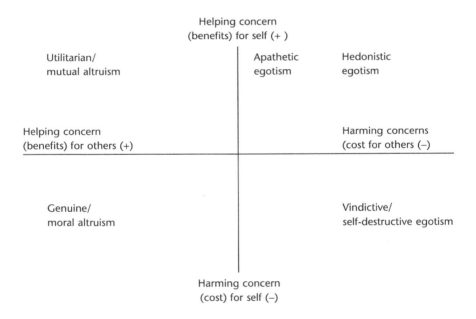

Figure 2.1   Forms of altruistic and egotistic behaviour
Source: Kanungo & Mendonca (1996); Reprinted with permission

The two dimensions are: behaviour reflecting (in its consequences) a concern for benefiting or harming others; and behaviour reflecting (in its consequences) a concern for benefiting or harming oneself. The two axes in Figure 2.1 represent these two dimensions, which proves useful to analyse the behaviours in the biblical story that introduced this section. For example, when a behaviour reflects a helping concern (or deriving benefits) for self but a harming concern for others, it represents what we call *hedonistic egotism* – as is the case with the behaviour of the thieves. Often, a behaviour reflects helping concern for oneself with no apparent concern for others, either actively providing help or causing harm to others. Such behaviour can be termed *apathetic egotism* and describes the behaviour of the priest and the Levite.

Egotistic behaviour can also take the form of *vindictive* or *self-destructive egotism*. It reflects a harming concern for both others and oneself. This behaviour is not found in our biblical story, but in personal and organizational contexts, an individual who exhibits such behaviour generally adopts an 'I will take you down with me' attitude. The violent manifestations of such behaviour in the workplace – as, for example, with disgruntled and dissatisfied employees gunning down their managers – is often reported in the media. It is, however, not uncommon to come across relatively mild forms of such behaviour in the workplace – for example, managers, motivated by vendetta, suppress critical information or are unwilling to surrender resources, even when they recognize that these actions would adversely affect both their own units as well as the organization.

In contrast to these forms of egotistic behaviour, altruistic behaviour always reflects a helping concern for others. When such a concern is combined with a concern for one's own self-interest, the behaviour can be called *utilitarian* or *mutual altruism*. The inn-keeper in the biblical story demonstrated utilitarian altruism because he helped the injured traveller after being assured of compensation by the Samaritan. The motivational basis of utilitarian altruism is the expectations about the mutually beneficial consequences of the obligatory behaviour. The last behaviour category depicted in Figure 2.1 reflects a helping concern for others without any regard for self-interest, even when such concern involves considerable personal sacrifice or inconvenience, that is, harming self-interest. This behaviour can be categorized as *genuine* or *moral altruism* – as demonstrated by the behaviour of the Samaritan. The primary motivational force behind moral altruism is the internalized social responsibility norms or moral imperatives. Moral philosophers may argue about different normative theories of ethics or morality. However, people in every part of the globe, in every culture, in every age – ancient, medieval, modern, or contemporary – will be unanimous in conceding that this Samaritan truly deserves the title of the 'good' Samaritan.

The values inherent in the choice of 'others before myself' or 'moral altruism' are universal and form part of the heritage of all cultures. To illustrate this point, we cite examples from two religious traditions and cultures – the West European and the Hindu; both have fundamentally different approaches to the sources of religious truth that illuminate the path to moral behaviour. The West European religious traditions have been formed by the thinking of both the Greeks and the Romans and by Judaism and Christianity. Hinduism – or, more appropriately, the Hindu view of life – is based on religious truths that have been expounded by the *rishiis* (the wise sages) and are contained essentially in the tales of two epics, the *Ramayana* and the *Mahabharata*. Despite these differences, we find interesting parallels in the hierarchy of values in relation to the 'self or other' question. In both religious cultures, the 'self or other' relationship can be considered at broadly three levels. The lowest level focuses on behaviours exclusively geared to the gratification of the self; for example, *eros* in Western traditions or *kama* in Hindu traditions. The next level corresponds to behaviours primarily motivated by familial considerations, helping those who are already close to you: *philia* in Western traditions or *prema* in Hindu traditions. The highest level consists of behaviours performed for the benefit of others, even if it comes at the cost of one's self: *agape* in Western traditions or *mokshya* in Hindu traditions.

Conclusion

Our review of the theories of ethics suggest that the personalist philosophy of Karol Wojtyla provides a sound foundation for developing appropriate moral principles and standards to judge morally right and morally wrong intentions and actions of leaders. The discussion in subsequent chapters will draw on these principles and standards.

Suggested questions for reflection

- What is a major difference in the method of moral reasoning between utilitarianism and Kant's idealism?
- What are some of the insights offered by personalism on the nature and uniqueness of the human person?
- Which of the following attitudes best serve both the individual good and the common good? Why?

  → conformism
  → non-involvement
  → opposition
  → solidarity

- What is altruism? What are the manifest behaviours of altruism?

---

3 Leadership theory and research: a brief overview

Synopsis

In this chapter we examine the leadership phenomenon through an overview of leadership theory and research from the point of view of social and organizational psychology. We examine the existing modal orientations in leadership theory and research on essentially three aspects: leader role behaviour, contingencies of leadership effectiveness, and the leader-follower influence process. We assess the limitations of the existing theoretical paradigms; and also examine the emerging trends – in particular, the neo-charismatic paradigm, which best responds to the needs of organizations in a highly turbulent environment, and in the context of increasing globalization of business and interdependence among nations. We discuss a representative formulation of the neo-charismatic paradigm – a three-stage model of charismatic or transformational leadership. The discussion describes the model: the behavioural components; the influence process; the attribution of charisma; and the outcomes of charismatic leadership behaviours.

Introduction

From time immemorial, leaders both mythical and historical have been celebrated in folklore, art, music, opera, and literature – statues, triumphal arches, mausoleums, and magnificent edifices have been built to honour them; cities, ships, aircraft, and even babies have been named after them. However, the leadership phenomenon seems to elude scholars, much to their bewilderment and frustration. The examination of leadership as a group and organizational phenomenon has been the focus of both theoretical and empirical analysis for more than half a century (Burns, 1978; Hollander, 1978; Bennis and Nanus, 1985; Bass, 1990a). Yet, in spite of the decades of research, our understanding of the leadership phenomenon remains incomplete.

Social scientists of many persuasions, including political scientists (Burns, 1978; Wilner, 1984), sociologists (Roberts, 1985; Bradley, 1987), organization theorists (Pfeffer, 1977; Nadler and Tushman, 1990), psychoanalysts (Zaleznik, 1990; Kets de Vries, 1994) and psychologists (Bass, 1990a; Hollander and Offermann, 1990), have contributed to the enigmatic nature of the leadership phenomenon by proposing various analytical frameworks and focusing on different content and process aspects of leadership in a wide range of contexts. These multidisciplinary approaches not only spoke in languages specific to their own disciplines – sometimes unintelligible to those of other disciplines – but also adopted diverse levels of analysis, micro and macro, individual and interactional, process and structure, to explain the constructs and processes related to leadership.

The resulting disparate, incomparable analytical treatments (see for example, Bryman, 1986; Hunt *et al.*, 1988; Yukl, 1998) and empirical attempts have provided conflicting evidence on the role of leadership in organizational and group performance, and this has obscured rather than facilitated our understanding of the phenomenon. At the conceptual level, there is the difficulty of developing integrative and reasonably comprehensive frameworks to understand the leadership phenomenon. At the empirical level, the ambiguity of research findings has led some to even question the usefulness of research endeavours in the leadership area. Researchers in both psychology and management (Pfeffer, 1977; Kerr and Jermier, 1978; Fiedler and Chemers, 1984; House, 1988a) have debated the issue of what precisely are the critical properties and processes of the leadership phenomenon, and whether leadership does or does not make a difference in explaining and predicting the success or failure of groups and organizations. Such attempts have neither produced a unifying and comprehensive theoretical framework (Bryman, 1986), nor have they succeeded in establishing empirically an unequivocal link between leadership and organizational and group performance (Thomas, 1988). Hence, we have several splinter theories of leadership and numerous empirical studies within each advocacy camp which have led many to describe this state of affairs as a 'crisis in leadership research' (Hunt *et al.*, 1988: 243).

Our purpose here is not to get entangled in the controversy of whether it is feasible or even worthwhile to study the leadership phenomenon, which has eluded us thus far. Although we recognize the importance of existing knowledge and the need to continue scientific research on leadership in order to better understand the phenomenon, we do not intend to present here an exhaustive review of the enormous psychological literature on the topic. Such reviews exist elsewhere (see, for example, Bass, 1990a; Yukl, 1998). Rather, the purpose of this chapter is to enhance our understanding of the leadership phenomenon by seeking answers to questions such as: What have we learned from the past leadership debates in the psychological literature? On which issues is there most agreement among researchers? What ought to be the future direction of leadership research in the field of organizational behaviour? The research in leadership has encompassed many disciplines, such as anthropology, sociology, and political science. Our focus will be restricted to leadership from the point of view of social and organizational psychology.

Towards this end, the objective of our analysis will be to: (1) identify some basic assumptions underlying leadership theory and research; (2) indicate the modal orientations in leadership paradigms reflected in the writings of social and organizational psychologists; (3) assess the limitations of these paradigms; (4) review the neo-charismatic paradigm – in particular, the behavioural components and leadership influence process of charismatic and transformational leadership. This four-fold analysis will provide a basis for an examination of the ethical implications in Chapters 4 and 5.

Basic assumptions underlying leadership theory and research

The theoretical frameworks and investigative strategies researchers adopt when they explore a behavioural phenomenon are to a large extent directed by their assumptions about the nature of that phenomenon. In fact, controversies and misunderstandings among researchers can often be traced to the failure to recognize that differences exist in respect of the implicit assumptions adopted in their studies; hence the need to be as explicit as possible about one's assumptions. For this reason, before we attempt to identify the modal orientations in leadership research, we start by explicitly stating the assumptions commonly held among behavioural scientists about leadership.

The first assumption is that researchers in social and organizational psychology have come to accept leadership as an organizational or group phenomenon. The phenomenon is observed as a *set of role behaviours* performed by an individual when there is a need to influence and coordinate the activities of group or organizational members towards the achievement of a common goal. This individual is called the 'leader', and the focus on behaviours can be said to be the behavioural approach to leadership. Before the behavioural approach, leadership was viewed in terms of the 'great man' or 'traits' theory of leadership, which essentially proposed that the success of a leader is to be attributed solely to his or her personality and physical traits or characteristics without regard to the situational context (Cowley, 1928). However, numerous studies have failed to identify such traits common to all leaders. The trait approach was considered too simplistic an explanation of the complex leadership phenomenon (Dorfman, 1994). Therefore, instead of studying leadership as a cluster of stable personality traits, in isolation from their context, today we view leadership as a set of role behaviours by individuals in the context of the group or organization to which they belong – behaviours such as: '... setting group goals, moving the group toward its goals, building cohesiveness of the group, and making resources available to the group' (Cartwright and Zander, 1968: 304).

From the description of leadership as a set of role behaviours in a group context, follows the second assumption that leadership is both a *relational* and an *attributional* phenomenon. Thus, it is assumed that leadership comes into being when followers perceive the leader's behaviour in a certain way, accept the leader's influence attempts, and then attribute leadership status to the individual. Without the followers' perceptions, acceptance, and attributions, the leadership phenomenon simply would not exist (Beckhard, 1996).

The third assumption is that leadership can be studied in terms of its *contents* and *processes*. The study of the content (or elements) of leadership seeks to identify: (a) the specific sets of leader role behaviours that serve to achieve the group's objectives by influencing the attitudes and behaviours of group members; and (b) the properties of followers and situations – such as the task, and the social climate – that facilitate or hinder the manifestation of leadership.

The study of leadership processes reveals the types of social influence processes that operate, and the psychological dynamics underlying them. More specifically, leadership implies the exercise of influence over others through the utilization of various bases of social power, reinforcers, tactics, and so on, in order to elicit the group members' compliance with certain norms and the commitment necessary to achieve the group's objectives (Kelman, 1958; French and Raven, 1959; Sims and Lorenzi, 1992).

The distinction between content and process in leadership research leads to the fourth assumption. It is that in order to understand the leadership phenomenon, one must analyse the properties of: (a) the basic *leadership elements* – the leader, the followers, the situational context; and (b) the major *relational processes* – the leader-follower influence process, the leader-context relational process, and the context-follower relational process (see Conger and Kanungo, 1988c, for this type of analysis of charismatic leadership).

The fifth and final assumption is that the role behaviours of a leader are intended to directly influence followers' attitudes and behaviours within the group or organizational context. Hence, *leadership effectiveness* should be measured in terms of the degree to which a leader promotes: (a) the instrumental attitudes and behaviours for the achievement of group objectives; (b) the followers' satisfaction with the task and context within which they operate; and (c) the followers' acceptance of the leader's influence. The followers' acceptance of the leader's influence is often manifested through the followers' emotional bond with the leader, by their attributions of favourable qualities to the leader, by their compliance behaviours, and by their commitment to the leader's attitudes and values. However, instead of these measures, leadership effectiveness is more often measured in terms of group or organizational productivity, such as '... profits, profits margin, sales increase, market share, sales relative to targeted sales, return on investment, productivity, cost per unit of output, costs in relation to budgeted expenditures' (Yukl, 1998: 6). We do not believe that such indices, however objective, are appropriate measures of a leader's influence or effectiveness because these indices depend not only on the followers' instrumental behaviour, but also on available environmental resources, technology, market conditions and so on, over which a leader may have little control.

Modal orientations in leadership paradigms

The modal orientation of past leadership research in both social and organizational psychology has been to address three specific issues related to constructs of the 'leader' and 'leadership effectiveness'. First, a concern for understanding the leader construct led researchers to identify *leader role behaviours* in groups. To understand the leadership effectiveness construct led to the second and third research issues. Specifically, the second research issue sought to identify the *contingencies of leadership effectiveness* by studying the interactions between role behaviours and the characteristics of followers and of the situational context. The third research issue focused on analysing the underlying mechanisms of the *leader-follower influence process* itself. We briefly discuss each of these modal trends.

Leader role behaviours

Early social psychological studies examined small groups – formal and informal, in both laboratory and field settings, to identify leader role behaviours. These studies (Bales and Slater, 1955; Fleishmann, Harris, and Burtt, 1955; Halpin and Winer, 1957; Cartwright and Zander, 1968) converged on the thesis that leadership role behaviours are functionally related to two broad group objectives: group maintenance and group task achievement. A group member, in an informal group, or an appointed leader, in a formal group, is perceived to be acting as a leader when he or she engages in activities which promote group maintenance and/or ensure task performance and goal achievement.

Following in this vein, later studies of supervision and leadership in organizations (Yukl, 1998) identified two major leadership roles: a consideration or people orientation role (social role), and an initiating structure or task orientation role (task role). In the people orientation role, the leader's behaviour is characterized by high sensitivity to the feelings of group members, mutual trust of and openness to members' suggestions. In the task-oriented role, the leader defines and structures tasks and roles of group members in order to achieve the goals of the group (Andriessen and Drenth, 1984). This two-dimensional approach greatly influenced management practice, as evidenced by the popularity of leadership training programmes such as the management grid (Blake and Mouton, 1964), which sought to identify the managers' predominant orientation – whether it was a task or a social orientation.

A third leadership role, related to decision-making, was identified by the work of Lewin and his associates (Lewin, Lippitt, and White, 1939; Lippitt and White, 1947). These studies examined the autocratic and democratic (or participative) leadership roles in groups and their impact on decision-making and decision implementation. In providing direction, in problem solving, or in providing interaction opportunities for group members, the leader could engage in either autocratic behaviour, by using leader's own individual resources, or in participative behaviour, by using the resources available among the group members.

As we can see from the above review, three leader role behaviours – social role, task role, and decision-making role – dominated leadership research from the 1940s until the 1980s.

Contingencies of leadership effectiveness

Building upon the two-dimensional approach to leader role behaviours, Fiedler and Chemers (1984) proposed the notion that a particular leader role, such as initiating structure versus consideration, was contingent upon the situational context for its effectiveness. They operationalized a model with two key leadership attributes termed as high and low LPC – that is, 'Least Preferred Coworker'. The high LPC resembled the social role, and low LPC resembled the task role. According to Fiedler's contingency model, in certain situations with certain types of tasks, follower attitudes, and position power, the low LPC leaders would be more effective than high LPC leaders; and vice versa. For example, in situations in which the task is highly structured, relations with subordinates are good, and the leader has substantial position power, the low LPC leader is the most effective. But, if the task is unstructured and the leader's position power is weak, then, despite the good relations with subordinates, the high LPC leader is more likely to be effective. Another contingency model using the two-dimensional approach was advanced by Hersey and Blanchard (1984). In a related approach, Kerr and Jermier (1978) identified two kinds of situational factors referred to as substitutes or neutralizers of leadership influence on subordinates. Their 'substitutes for leadership' specify a set of characteristics of followers, tasks, and organizational contexts that reduce or nullify the effects of relationship-oriented and task-oriented leadership roles. In these situations, highly experienced subordinates or an unambiguous task might substitute for the need for leadership.

One additional school of contingency theorists explored the effects of autocratic, consultative and participative leadership behaviour on the effectiveness of a leader in achieving group objectives. This line of research was initiated by the classic studies of autocratic and democratic leadership by Lewin and his associates (Lewin, Lippitt, and White, 1939; Lippitt and White, 1947). Their published findings in both the social psychological and organizational behaviour literature (Tannenbaum and Schmidt, 1958; Vroom and Yetton, 1973) suggested that the extent to which a leader involved followers in decision-making was critical to leadership effectiveness. Using a continuum of decision-making styles – from autocratic to consultative to participative – they identified the decision-making style that was most appropriate to the characteristics of the situation, keeping in mind both the tasks and the followers. For example, when a decision is important and subordinates possess relevant knowledge and information lacked by the leader, an autocratic decision would be inappropriate (Vroom and Yetton, 1973).

Leader-follower influence process

How and why are leaders effective in influencing their followers? This question was explored from three different theoretical perspectives which examined the psychological mechanisms that explain the linkage between the leader's role behaviour and the followers' compliance and commitment to achieving group or organizational objectives. These perspectives, discussed below, are: (a) the bases of social power (Dahl, 1957; French and Raven, 1959); (b) the nature of social exchange (Blau, 1974; Hollander, 1979); and (c) the motivational dynamics (Evans, 1970; House, 1971; Luthans and Kreitner, 1975).

According to Cartwright (1965), the leader's effectiveness in influencing followers stems from the followers' perception that the leader possesses and controls resources valued by followers. Most studies of leadership effectiveness from the perspective of 'basis of social power' (Student, 1968; Kanungo, 1977) have used French and Raven's (1959) formulation of five kinds of resources that form the bases of social power – the reward, coercive, legal, expert and referent power bases. The first three power bases – reward, coercive, legal – are often assumed to stem from the leader's formal authority position within a group or an organization; hence, referred to as position power bases. The last two power bases – expert, referent – are considered as residing in the leader's idiosyncratic ways of influencing followers; hence, termed as personal power or idiosyncratic power bases. The use of personal power by a leader has an incremental influence on followers (Katz and Kahn, 1978) over and above the influence that results from the use of the leader's position power. Such incremental influence on performance is reflected in the followers' performance beyond the organizationally prescribed performance expectations. The role of the personal power base in influencing followers has become a central issue in charismatic and transformational leadership, discussed later.

In the perspective of the social exchange theory (Blau, 1974), leaders gain status and influence over group members in return for demonstrating task competence and loyalty to the group. Hollander and Offermann (1990) call this type of explanation 'a process-oriented transactional approach to leadership . . . It emphasizes the implicit social exchange or transaction over time that exists between the leaders and followers, including reciprocal influence and interpersonal perception' (p. 181). Using this approach, Hollander (1958, 1986) had advanced the 'idiosyncratic credit' model of leadership that explains why the innovative ideas of leaders gain acceptance among followers. According to this model, leaders earn such credits from followers' perceptions that these innovative ideas reflect their leaders' competence, good judgement and loyalty. For example, when followers see that their leader's innovative ideas are successful, then their trust in the leader's expertise is confirmed. Hence, followers are more likely to suspend their judgement and more readily accept the leader's innovative ideas. As the leader's successes increase, so do the idiosyncratic credits. Leaders can then utilize these credits which, in effect, represent the followers' trust, in order to influence followers' compliance and commitment to innovative goals.

Finally, leaders' influence on followers has also been explained by analysing the 'motivational dynamics' which govern follower satisfaction and performance. A path-goal theory of leadership, first proposed by Evans (1970) and later advanced by House (1971), used the expectancy theory of motivation to explain leadership effectiveness. According to House and his associates (House and Dessler, 1974; House and Mitchell, 1974), each of the four types of leadership role behaviour such as directive, achievement-oriented, supportive, and participative, influences followers by increasing the personal pay-offs to them for group task accomplishments and 'making the path to these payoffs easier to travel by clarifying it, reducing roadblocks and pitfalls, and increasing the opportunities for personal satisfaction en route' (House, 1971: 324). Oldham (1976) also suggested a similar motivational explanation for the effectiveness of leadership activities when he observes that the leaders' actions of rewarding, setting goals, designing job and feedback systems, and so on enhance the followers' motivation. Other researchers (Sims, 1977; Podsakoff, Todor and Skov, 1982) have explained leadership effectiveness in terms of the behaviour modification principles of contingent reinforcement. Maintaining influence over followers through the use of contingent reinforcement has also been interpreted as a form of transactional leadership (Avolio and Bass, 1988).

In summary, these modal trends have led to a focus on three major leadership role dimensions: (1) a people-concern that manifests itself in a relationship orientation, and consideration and supportive activities; (2) a task-concern which focuses on achievement orientation, and activities that emphasize initiating structure, goal setting, and facilitating task performance; and (3) a concern for making and implementing decisions, which includes characteristics such as facilitating interaction, and determination of the appropriateness of styles that range from autocratic and directive to consultative and participative. These specific role dimensions have been studied in situational contexts involving varied characteristics of three distinct elements: tasks, followers, groups or organizations. Most contingency theories of leadership consider these three elements as possible contingencies for understanding leadership effectiveness.

Finally, the nature of the leader-follower influence process is also understood in terms of the three theoretical perspectives: control over valued resources, social exchange processes, and motivational dynamics. During the last quarter of a century, leadership contingency models dealing with the three behaviour dimensions, the three situational elements, and the three classes of explanations discussed above have dominated the scientific literature, both in the East (Sinha, 1980; Misumi, 1988) and the West (Fiedler, 1967; Heller, 1971; House, 1971; Vroom and Yetton, 1973).

Limitations of the modal orientations

A conception of leadership in terms of the models, reviewed in the previous section, have been considered to be too narrow and sterile (Hunt, 1991). As Bass and Avolio (1993) point out, 'Initiation and consideration were not sufficient to explain the full range of leadership behaviours commonly associated with the best and also the worst leaders' (p. 50). Past leadership research ignored certain core aspects of leadership role activities, such as the critical assessment of the environment and status quo; formulation and articulation of a future vision; building of trust and credibility in the minds of followers in order to develop their commitment to the vision. There is also inadequate attention to the study of followers' motivations in submitting to their leaders. 'Although the study of leadership has always presumed the existence of followers, their roles were viewed as essentially passive' (Hollander and Offermann, 1990: 182).

There are three main reasons for the limitations of the existing models and related research strategies. First, these are based principally on small groups – in a laboratory or in organizations. This limited focus would not capture certain elements of leadership – such as the formulation of a mission or a strategic vision, as observed in large corporations or in religious, social and political organizations. Second, the studies of supervision in organizations have always used follower attitudes and behaviours as dependent

variables, rather than as antecedents or explanations for the leadership phenomena. Consequently, these studies have neglected to utilize the follower-
centred approaches and, as a result, understanding of leadership as an attributional process remains incomplete. Third, most leadership studies in the
organizational contexts have been studies of supervision, with an emphasis
on the day-to-day routine maintenance of the status quo, rather than the true
phenomenon of future leadership as observed in society. The core element of
supervision or managership is the effective maintenance of the status quo,
whereas a core element of leadership is to effectively bring about improve-
ments, changes and transformations in the existing system and in its
members.

Emerging trends in leadership research

For all the foregoing reasons, leadership studies need to shift from the current
preoccupation with task, people, and participative orientations to the crucial
behaviours observed in leaders who bring about profound changes in both
the organizations and in their members – behaviours such as visioning, articulating a vision, and developing strategies to achieve the vision (Conger
and Kanungo, 1988a; Bass, 1990). Likewise, more attention needs to be paid
to the follower-centred approaches with an emphasis on follower perceptions
and attributions in the leader-follower dynamics (Hollander and Offerman,
1990). The needed paradigm shift is already occurring, as can be seen from the
recent emergence of interest in charismatic and transformational leadership
(Conger and Kanungo, 1987; Conger, 1989a; Bass and Avolio, 1993; House,
1995; Kanungo and Mendonca, 1996a, 1996b), follower attributions (Meindl
et al., 1985), and empowerment (Conger and Kanungo, 1988c; Hollander and
Offermann, 1990; Thomas and Velthouse, 1990; Spreitzer, 1995, 1996).

   The emerging trend in leadership research – to move beyond the task,
social, and participative leadership roles to other roles – is called the neo-
charismatic paradigm (House, 1995). The neo-charismatic paradigm recognizes that past leadership research has neglected to study two of the most
important leadership behaviours as defined by Cartwright and Zander (1968):
'setting group goals' and 'moving the group toward its goals' (p. 304). Through
these activities, leaders bring about changes in groups and organizations and
transform their members' beliefs and values. The neo-charismatic paradigm
(House, 1995) asserts that leaders are visionary (in the sense that they set
future goals for the organization) and induce significant organizational
change. Several behavioural theories have been proposed to explain the
charismatic leadership role under this neo-charismatic paradigm (House,
1977; Bass, 1985; Conger and Kanungo, 1987; Sashkin, 1988).

   We now explore a representative formulation of the neo-charismatic paradigm, the Conger-Kanungo Model of Charismatic Leadership. The results of six studies – in different organizational contexts and conducted in three different countries (Canada, India, the USA) – have established the validity of the model (Conger and Kanungo, 1998). The sections that follow describe the model – the behavioural components, the influence process, the attribution of charisma, and the outcomes of charismatic leadership behaviour as formulated by Conger and Kanungo (1998).

Conger-Kanungo Model of Charismatic Leadership (behavioural components)

The model builds on the idea that charismatic leadership is an attribution based on followers' perceptions of their leader's behaviour – in the three stages of the model – see Figure 3.1. The model views charismatic leaders as moving organizational members from an existing state towards a desired future state. In this section, we describe the behaviours in each stage; this set of behaviours may be regarded as the 'content' of charismatic leadership – what charismatic leaders do. In order to address these behavioural components in a leader's charismatic role, a valid and reliable questionnaire measure has been developed (Conger, Kanungo, Menon and Mathur, 1997; Conger, Kanungo and Menon, 2000). The items in this questionnaire are presented in Appendix I.

Stage 1: Evaluation of the status quo

In this stage, charismatic leaders critically evaluate the status quo in order to identify the deficiencies and the poorly exploited opportunities as well as the constraints in the environment. Towards this end, charismatic leaders are highly sensitive to both the social and physical environments in which they operate. They will take all the means for realistic assessment, including internal and external sources. When leaders fail to assess properly the constraints in the environment or the availability of resources, their strategies and actions may not achieve the organizational objectives. For this reason, the knowledge, experience, and expertise of the leader become critical. The charismatic leader must also be sensitive to both the abilities and the emotional needs of followers – the most important resources for attaining organizational goals. The leader's assessment of environmental resources and constraints, as well as the needs and aspirations of the followers, is critical before planning courses of action.

Because of their emphasis on deficiencies in the system and their high levels of intolerance for them, charismatic leaders are always seen as organizational reformers or entrepreneurs. In other words, they act as agents of

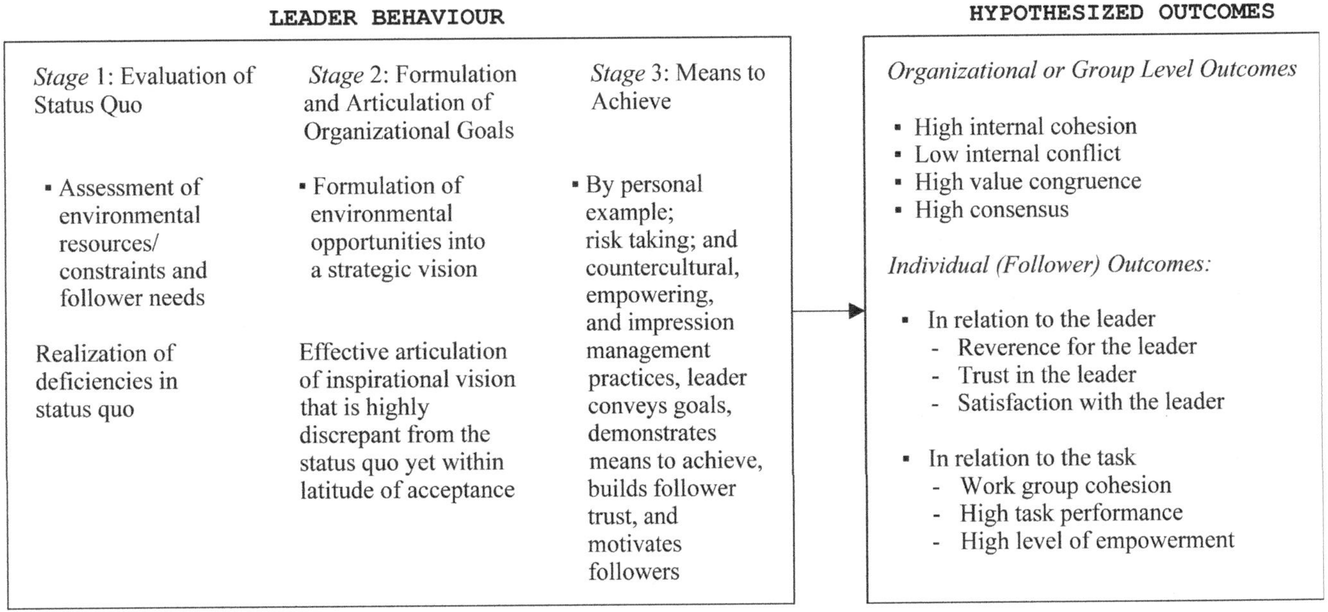

LEADER BEHAVIOUR

Stage 1: Evaluation of Status Quo

- Assessment of environmental resources/ constraints and follower needs

Realization of deficiencies in status quo

Stage 2: Formulation and Articulation of Organizational Goals

- Formulation of environmental opportunities into a strategic vision

Effective articulation of inspirational vision that is highly discrepant from the status quo yet within latitude of acceptance

Stage 3: Means to Achieve

- By personal example; risk taking; and countercultural, empowering, and impression management practices, leader conveys goals, demonstrates means to achieve, builds follower trust, and motivates followers

HYPOTHESIZED OUTCOMES

Organizational or Group Level Outcomes

- High internal cohesion
- Low internal conflict
- High value congruence
- High consensus

Individual (Follower) Outcomes:

- In relation to the leader
  - Reverence for the leader
  - Trust in the leader
  - Satisfaction with the leader

- In relation to the task
  - Work group cohesion
  - High task performance
  - High level of empowerment

Figure 3.1 A Stage Model of Charismatic Leadership

Source: Conger and Kanungo (1998), Reprinted with permission

innovative and radical change. The attribution of charisma, however, is dependent not on the outcome of change but simply on the actions taken to bring about change or reform.

Charismatic leaders differ from administrators and supervisors from the perspective of managing and fostering change. Since administrators generally act as caretakers, they have little interest in significant organizational change. When they may advocate change, the change is usually incremental and within the bounds of the status quo. Charismatic leaders, on the other hand, seek radical reforms for the achievement of their idealized goals and the transformation of their followers. For this reason, these behaviours are necessary and supporting features of charismatic leaders.

Stage 2: Formulation and articulation of the future vision

After assessing the environment, charismatic leaders formulate and articulate an idealized vision – the future goals for achieving the organization's objectives. Charismatic leaders are often characterized by a sense of strategic vision (Marcus, 1961; Dow, 1969; Berlew, 1974; Zaleznik and Kets de Vries, 1975; Willner, 1984; Conger, 1985; Bass and Avolio, 1993; House, 1995).

The more idealized the future goal advocated by the leader, the more discrepant it becomes in relation to the status quo. The greater the discrepancy from the status quo, the more likely the followers' attribution that the leader has extraordinary vision, not just an ordinary goal. Also, a very discrepant and idealized goal provides followers a sense of challenge and a motivating force for change. The attitude change literature suggests that a maximum discrepant position within the latitude of acceptance puts the greatest amount of pressure on followers to change their attitudes (Hovland and Pritzker, 1957; Petty and Cacioppo, 1981). The idealized goal, despite its extreme discrepancy, tends to be within the latitude of acceptance when it is articulated to represent a perspective shared by the followers and promises to meet their hopes and aspirations. Followers attribute charisma to leaders when their vision represents an embodiment of a perspective shared by followers in an idealized form. The vision also reinforces the followers' sense of collective identity that facilitates the followers placing the interests of the organization over their own interests – even at personal cost (Shamir, House, and Arthur, 1993).

To be charismatic, leaders must be able to articulate their visions and strategies for action in effective ways so as to influence their followers. Here, articulation involves two separate processes: articulation of the context and articulation of the leader's motivation to lead. Effective articulation of the context requires in essence that the status quo is presented as intolerable and the vision as the most attractive and attainable alternative which remedies the deficiencies and exploits the opportunities – in the context of the available resources and constraints. For effective articulation of the leaders' motivation to lead, charismatic leaders use expressive modes of action – both verbal and non-verbal, to demonstrate their convictions, self-confidence, and dedication to the vision.

Stage 3: Achieving the vision

In the final stage of the leadership process, effective leaders engage in behaviours which build in followers a trust in the leader's vision – more specifically, in the leader's abilities to achieve the organization's goals necessary to realize the vision. They do this through personal example and risk-taking, as well as through unconventional expertise. Generally, leaders are perceived as trustworthy when they advocate their position in a disinterested and selfless manner and demonstrate a concern for followers' needs rather than their own self-interest (Walster, Aronson, and Abrahams, 1966). For this purpose, they must engage in exemplary acts that are perceived by followers as involving great personal risk, cost, and energy (Friedland, 1964). Acts of personal risk might include the possible loss of personal finances, the possibility of being fired or demoted, and the potential loss of formal or informal status, power, authority, and credibility. When leaders demonstrate that they are indefatigable workers prepared to take on high personal risks or incur high personal costs to achieve their shared vision, the more they reflect charisma in the sense of being worthy of complete trust.

Charismatic leaders also build trust in the vision when they are seen by followers to be knowledgeable and experts in their areas of influence. Some degree of demonstrated expertise, such as reflected in successes in the past, may be a necessary condition for the attribution of charisma (Weber, 1947; Conger, 1989a). Furthermore, it is hypothesized that the attribution of charisma generally is influenced by the expertise of leaders in two areas. First, charismatic leaders use their expertise in demonstrating the inadequacy of the traditional technology, rules, and regulations of the status quo as a means of achieving the shared vision (Weber, 1947). Second, charismatic leaders show an expertise in devising effective but unconventional strategies and plans of action (Conger, 1985). Leaders are also perceived as charismatic when they reveal expertise through the use of unconventional or countercultural means. Iacocca's use of government-backed loans, money back guarantees on cars, union representation on the board, and advertisements featuring himself are examples of unconventional strategic actions in the automobile industry. The leaders' unconventional behaviours evoke in their followers emotional responses of surprise and admiration and lead to a dispositional attribution of charisma.

Conger-Kanungo Model of Charismatic Leadership (influence process)

The previous section described the 'content' of charismatic leadership – what leaders do. The influence process adopted by the leader constitutes the 'process', or how and why the leader's behaviour is effective in influencing followers. According to Burns (1978), there are basically two influence processes, or ways of influencing followers, that are available to leaders. These are the transactional influence processes and the transformational influence processes.

In the transactional influence process, the leader ensures that followers perform the required behaviours through the use of rewards and sanctions. The transactional mode of exercising leadership influence is implicit in the major leadership roles of: the people orientation or the social role; the task orientation or the task role, and the participative role. In the transformational influence process, the leader works to bring about a change in the followers' attitudes and values as the leader moves the organization towards its goals in realization of the vision. The leadership influence processes, transactional and transformational, and related influence strategies, are discussed at length in Chapter 4, along with the ethical implications of these processes.

Attribution of charisma

The three major features of the behavioural components in each stage of the model are: high environmental sensitivity in relation to the status quo in stage one; formulation and articulation of the vision in stage two; devising unconventional means to achieve the vision in stage three. The likelihood of followers attributing charisma to a leader will depend on: (a) the number of behavioural components manifested in a leader's behaviour; (b) the level of intensity of each component as expressed in a leader's behaviour; and (c) the level of saliency or importance of individual components as determined by the existing situation and the level of follower proximity to the leader.

Thus, a leader who is skilful only at detecting deficiencies in the status quo is less likely to be seen as charismatic than one who not only detects deficiencies but also formulates future visions, articulates them, and devises unconventional means for achieving them. Leaders who engage in advocating highly discrepant and idealized visions and use highly unconventional means to achieve these visions are more likely to be perceived as charismatic. Likewise, leaders who express high personal commitment to an objective, who take high personal risk, and who use intense articulation techniques are more likely to be perceived as charismatic.

Followers are more likely to attribute charisma to a leader when they perceive his or her behaviour to be contextually appropriate and/or in congruence with their own values. Thus, in a traditional organizational culture that subscribes to conservative modes of behaviour among employees and the use of conventional means to achieve organizational objectives, leaders who engage in excessive unconventional behaviour may be viewed more as deviants than as charismatic figures.

Finally, proximity to the leader may influence the importance of certain behavioural components in attributions of charisma. For example, the components that influence follower attributions of charisma among a close circle of followers having direct contact with the leader may differ from those that influence attributions among a larger group of followers who have no direct contact with the leader.

Outcomes of charismatic leadership behaviour

The outcomes of the charismatic leadership behaviours can be observed either in terms of the end results for the organization, such as the objective indexes of return on investment, units produced, cost per unit, or cost savings, or in terms of follower outcomes, such as changes in follower beliefs, attitudes, and behaviour. However, as noted earlier, the effects on followers are the more appropriate measures of leadership effectiveness, because the objective indexes of end results often depend not only on followers' instrumental behaviour but also on other environmental contingencies over which leaders have little control. The hypothesized outcomes (Conger and Kanungo, 1998) are presented in Figure 3.1.

At the aggregate level, charismatic leadership behaviours will result in high internal cohesion, low internal conflict, high value congruence, and high consensus. Under a charismatic leader, there will be a greater degree of sharing of the vision and a greater degree of agreement with respect to the means for achieving the vision. At the individual level, followers' outcomes can be assessed in two ways: the followers' behaviours and attitudes toward the leader and toward the task. With respect to followers' relations with the charismatic leader, followers will show a high degree of reverence for the leader, a high degree of trust in the leader, and a high level of satisfaction with the leader. With respect to the followers' relations to the task, followers will show a high degree of cohesion with the work group, a high level of task performance, and a high level of feeling empowered within the organization to accomplish tasks (Conger, Kanungo and Menon, 2000).

Conclusion

Conger and Kanungo (1998) observed that charismatic leadership '... has at times produced disastrous outcomes for both followers and organizations' (p. 211). This is due to factors such as flawed vision, dysfunctional relations with followers, and succession challenges. The shadow side of charisma raises the important issue of the ethical standards of a 'good' leader. In his address to the Denver Rotary Club, Charles Chaput addressed this question.

> What makes a good leader? Two things: character and competence. You need the professional skills necessary for the task; that's competence. And you need the moral conscience to use those skills properly; that's character. A good leader creates the vision that other people can believe in and build together. And a good character always acts honestly ... Even more importantly, a good leader will put the needs of his people before his own. (2002: 1)

The nature of ethical leadership, explored at some length in Chapters 4 and 5, based on moral principles, indicates that the ethical leader strives to place 'others before self'. This strong altruistic value and orientation manifests itself on three dimensions: the leader's motives; the leader's influence strategies; and the leader's character formation. Hence, the leadership behaviours in the three-stage Conger-Kanungo Charismatic Model will be effective only to the extent that leaders perform these behaviours with an altruistic intent – to serve and benefit the organization and its members. Leadership effectiveness is greater and more enduring when leaders adopt the transformational influence process, rather than the transactional influence process, because the means, inherent in this process, such as followers' empowerment and related strategies, reflect the altruistic value and orientation. The leader's motives and influence strategies are the fruits of the leader's character. Therefore, it is inevitable that ethical leaders will tap the sources necessary, including practice of the virtues, to form their character.

Suggested questions for reflection

- In what way is the neo-charismatic paradigm a significant improvement over the past leadership research?
- With reference to the Conger-Kanungo Model of Charismatic Leadership:

  → what are the behaviours in each stage of the model?
  → what are the hypothesized outcomes of the model?
  → what are the three major features of the behavioural components which are most likely to make the followers attribute charisma to the leader?

- Is charismatic leadership an inherent quality or can it be learned?

4 The ethical dimensions of leadership: the leader's motives, influence strategies and character

Synopsis

In this chapter, we draw on altruism, a principle of moral behaviour, developed in Chapter 2, to explore the ethical dimensions of leadership as it relates to the leader's motives, the leader's influence strategies, and the leader's character. We discuss how leadership is effective when the leader's intent and influence strategies, in each of the three stages of the charismatic leadership model, reflect the altruistic value and orientation. In order to meet the demands of ethical leadership, we also highlight the fundamental importance of character formation, which is discussed at length in the next chapter.

Introduction

The several examples cited in the first chapter clearly demonstrate that when leaders compromise their ethical standards they do harm, often irreparable, in terms of the immediate physical and moral suffering to others within and outside the organization. They also create an atmosphere of ethical cynicism which is not conducive to forming a sound sense and understanding of the need for ethics and ethical behaviour. It is not uncommon for many in business to regard 'business ethics' as an oxymoron. Effective organizational leaders need ethics as fish need water, and human beings need air.

In Chapter 2, our exploration of the different ethical theories concluded that personalist philosophy is indeed a solid foundation for the moral life – in particular, for altruism as a principle of moral behaviour. In this chapter, we draw on altruism to discuss the ethical dimensions of ethical leadership as it relates to the leader's motives, the leader's influence strategies, and the leader's character.

The ethical dimensions of the leader's motives

Why is it essential for leaders to be altruistic?

In our discussion on the modal orientations of leadership in Chapter 3, we identified the effective organizational leader role as being one which fundamentally involves moving the organization from the status quo to a future desired goal. For this purpose, the charismatic leader performs a set of behaviours in three stages. These behaviours should provide direction, engender trust, and stimulate motivation in the followers to engage in activities that would achieve the vision. Now, if we analyse the leader's behaviours in the three stages in terms of the altruistic-egotistical dimensions, we can readily conclude that these behavioural attributes can only be demonstrated by a leader who is motivated by a high degree of moral altruism.

Thus, the typical behaviours in the first stage – the environmental assessment stage – are characterized by a heightened sensitivity to environmental opportunities and constraints, and to the needs of the followers. A leader whose gaze and focus is turned inwards, to his or her concerns and interests, which become the all-consuming passion and obsession, is prevented from being open and sensitive to others. Such a leader might be dissatisfied with the status quo and present proposals to change it. But these proposals, even though they constitute a radical reform of the status quo, will not be well received by the followers to the degree that the leader's self-orientation would not consider the followers' needs and aspirations. In contrast, a concern for the welfare of the organization and its members is the primary preoccupation which underlies the behaviours demanded of the charismatic leadership role from the very beginning of the charismatic leadership process. For this reason, managers in a charismatic leadership role are more likely to be perceived by followers both as stern critics of the status quo and as benevolent reformers or agents of radical change.

In the second stage – that is, the vision formulation and articulation stage – the critical behaviours of the charismatic leadership role are: the formulation of a shared, but idealized future vision, and the effective articulation of this vision in an inspirational manner. The focus of both sets of behaviours is 'others' – that is, the followers. The vision is undoubtedly the product of the leader's efforts in the environmental assessment stage. One might say that it is the expression of the person's beliefs and values, ideas and ideals, and unusual or creative discernment or perception of the opportunities which the organization can seize upon. Viewed in this way, the formulation of the vision appears to be very much the fruit of an individual's efforts. However, the realization of the idealized vision depends to a large extent on the followers' perception that it is a 'shared' vision.

It is important to explore the notions of 'shared', 'idealized' vision. As alluded to previously, a shared vision is one which embodies the perspective of the followers and, in effect, meets their needs and aspirations. The idealized characteristic can be said to take the vision a big step further. It creates in followers an awakening, a realization that the vision expresses their most profound yearnings for a state which, until now, they could not meaningfully articulate and, much less, believe to be possible. When leaders advocate an idealized vision or future goal for the organization, and influence followers to move towards it, they assume considerable personal risks. Their willingness to take these risks is largely prompted by a sense of altruistic mission. On the other hand, those who work to maintain the status quo when the interests and needs of the organization and its members demand change often do so in order to avoid the personal risks of change, and to cling on to the benefits, power, and influence which the status quo confers on them. In this case, we see that the desire to preserve one's self-interest clearly overrides the concern for the interests of others.

Furthermore, the charismatic leader's effectiveness in this stage depends equally upon the articulation of the vision. Since, as just discussed, the vision touches the very core of the followers' thoughts, feelings, and aspirations, the leader should communicate it in a manner that followers perceive to be genuinely natural, without any affectation or the use of gimmicks in its presentation. Clearly, a leader who is not motivated by a passionate and sincere care and concern, as well as a deep and abiding respect for others, will experience great difficulty in formulating and articulating the vision with the desired characteristics. Although effective organizational leaders engage in inspirational articulation of the idealized vision which reflects their altruistic motives, they also express them in several other ways. They express their strong beliefs in their own capability and in the capabilities of their followers to realize the vision. Through the expression of such beliefs, the leaders demonstrate their trust and confidence in their followers. It also provides followers with opportunities to assess the leaders' selfless commitment to the vision. When followers perceive that the leader does not trust them and does not show confidence in their capabilities, that the leader is more concerned with protecting his or her interests, then the articulation, however inspirational it might sound, will not cause the leader to be effective.

The focus on 'others' is much more evident in the third stage – that is, the implementation stage. The underlying intent of the behaviours in this stage is to motivate followers to achieve the vision by empowering them and developing their trust in the leader and the vision. For this purpose, the leader engages in modelling or exemplary acts, innovative and unconventional, which often involve great personal risks and sacrifices (Conger and Kanungo, 1988b, 1998). The inconvenience and pain, and even the losses, experienced by the leader in this process have to be perceived by the followers as more than an exercise in the satisfaction of the leader's masochistic desires. Rather, the followers must perceive these acts to be rooted in the leader's sincere desire to move followers towards the attainment of the shared vision. The leader also provides verbal encouragement and assistance in solving problems so that the followers may develop the necessary task-related self-efficacy, self-confidence and self-reliance. In order to ensure and encourage the personal growth and development of the followers, effective leaders adopt empowerment strategies to influence followers, whereas ineffective leaders have resort to control strategies. The nature and effects of these influence processes and their ethical implications will be discussed in the next chapter.

The preceding brief discussion of the leader's motivation in the three stages of the charismatic leadership process suggests that the behavioural attributes which are absolute imperatives for effective leadership can only be demonstrated by a leader who is motivated by a high degree of moral altruism. In other words, the satisfaction of the individual's altruistic need is the paramount condition for effective leadership. However, the existing leadership literature seems to ignore the altruistic need, and instead suggests that effective leadership is motivated by a set of other needs such as the need for affiliation, the need for power, and for achievement (McClelland and Burnham, 1995). These needs have played a critical role in leader motivation in the different modal orientations of leadership discussed in the previous chapter. For example, the social leadership role is motivated by a need for affiliation; the task leadership role is motivated by needs for power and achievement; the autocratic-participative leadership role is motivated by needs for power, achievement, and affiliation. Such a limited focus on the motivational dynamics of leadership has had two undesirable consequences. First, it ignored the more profound motive of altruism which is *the* critical ingredient of effective leadership. The second consequence follows from the first – by ignoring the altruistic motive, the discussion and study of the leadership phenomenon essentially avoided the moral and ethical issues that are involved in leadership.

We do recognize that it is appropriate and proper to study leadership behaviour as being caused by a set of needs, such as the needs for power, achievement, affiliation. In fact, without studying the overt behaviours generated by these needs, it might not be possible to obtain, at least, an initial understanding of the basis of effective leadership. However, it is necessary to probe further whether these needs do, by themselves, provide a reasonably comprehensive understanding of the motivational dynamics of leadership. Our thesis is that these needs explain the basis of effective leadership only to the extent that they are a manifestation of the overarching altruistic need. Stated differently, the affiliative, power, and achievement needs might be viewed as the *operative* needs which provide a starting point to understanding leadership role effectiveness; whereas, it is the presence of the deeper, *underlying* altruistic motive which better explains leader effectiveness. It is our intention to show that leader behaviours are ineffective when guided solely by one or more of these needs with a total disregard for altruism. On the other hand, leader behaviours are effective when motivated by these needs as an operative manifestation or expression of altruism.

The need for affiliation is dominant in the motivation of the social-oriented leader. Leaders who are high on affiliation motivation regard warm and friendly relationships with their followers as extremely important and, therefore, make considerable effort to be sensitive to followers' feelings and to conform to their wishes. These characteristics of the need for affiliation would suggest a concern for others and, hence, are compatible with the character-istics of the altruistic motive. However, Boyatzis (1973) posited two mani-festations of the need for affiliation. One is 'avoidance' affiliation; the other is 'approach' affiliation. Avoidance affiliation is '. . . a concern with the maintenance of relationships, and a fear of rejection and being left alone'; and approach affiliation is '. . . a concern with the establishment of "love" relationships' (Boyatzis, 1973: 270). Individuals high on avoidance affiliation correspond to those with a need for 'D-love' (deficiency-love, love need, selfish love) described by Maslow (1973: 249). The underlying motivation of these individuals' concern for others is to gain others' approval, to demon-strate their importance to others, and to develop their own self-worth. In essence, '. . . their strongest drive is to be liked' (McClelland and Burnham, 1995: 128). Individuals high on approach affiliation are similar to those with a need for 'B-love' (love for the Being of another person, unneeded love, unselfish love) described by Maslow (1973: 249). The approach affiliation individuals are motivated primarily by a genuine interest in others.

In the organizational context, Boyatzis (1982) viewed avoidance af-filiation as 'affiliative assurance', and approach affiliation as 'affiliative in-terest'. Individuals high on 'affiliative assurance' emphasize relationships to protect one's self. It has its origin in the individuals' sense of insecurity, and manifests itself in non-interfering and easy-to-get-along behaviours even when the job situation demands otherwise. For example, managers high on affiliative assurance are reluctant to give negative feedback to their sub-ordinates, yield to employee requests for the sole reason of not wanting to incur the employee's displeasure and without regard to the effect of their behaviour on the need for equity, due process, and order in the workplace. The interpersonal relations motivated by affiliative assurance produce low employee morale and defensive feelings, which invariably '. . . leaves em-ployees feeling weak, irresponsible, and without a sense of what might hap-pen next, of where they stand in relation to their manager, or even of what they ought to be doing' (McClelland and Burnham, 1995: 129). On the other hand, individuals high on 'affiliative interest' emphasize relationships in a manner that is consistent with the demands of the job tasks. It has its origin in the individuals' recognition that uncertainty pervades the workplace, and affiliative interest manifests itself in helpful but task-oriented information-seeking and interventions to reduce uncertainty and solve task-related problems. Affiliative interest demonstrates a high degree of 'interpersonal competence'. Managers who are high on affiliative interest relate to others with the full recognition that they are individual persons with ideas and resources and that they are partners in the problem-solving and related activities necessary for attaining task objectives (Moment and Zaleznik, cited in Litwin and Stringer, 1968). Consequently, supportive feelings permeate the interpersonal relations motivated by affiliative interest.

In the light of the preceding discussion, it is clear that the motivation of organizational leaders who are high on affiliative assurance is not only incompatible with the motivation which underlies moral altruism, but is also diametrically opposed to it; the motive underlying affiliative assurance is self-centric. On the other hand, the motivation of organizational leaders who are high on affiliative interest is other-centric and consistent with and conducive to motivation underlying moral altruism. The success or effectiveness of leaders who are high on affiliative interest relative to those high on affiliative assurance highlights the fact that the affiliative interest motivation exhibits to a considerable degree the underlying altruistic motive.

When one thinks of a leader, the notion that immediately comes to mind is 'power'. Undeniably, the power motivation or a high need for power has driven many a leader. Power, particularly in a democracy, has a very unfavourable press. The very mention of the word seems to evoke images of ruthless oppression and devious manipulation of human beings. It is, therefore, not surprising if the need for power seems as remote from the altruistic motive or behaviour as night is from day. However, a closer examination of this phenomenon reveals that there are, similar to the affiliation motivation, two types of power motivations. In one case, the leader is motivated by power for personal aggrandizement; in the other case, the leader is motivated by the power to serve the purpose of the institution. McClelland and Burnham (1995) term the former as the *personal power need* and the latter as the *institutional power need*.

Before we proceed further with the discussion, it is useful to note the difference between personal and institutional power needs, as suggested by McClelland and his associates, and the concepts of personal and position *power base*, derived from French and Raven's (1959) work on bases or sources of power, referred to in Chapter 3. The need for power – be it personal or institutional – triggers or motivates the leader to exercise influence or control over the followers. The leader's power base – be it personal or position – becomes the source of the resources which the leader can draw upon in order to exercise influence or control over the followers. Thus, the need for power provides the motivation for the exercise of influence, whereas the power base is the means which will be used for this purpose. In a sense, the need for power explains why influence or control is exercised; and the power base explains how it is exercised. Although these concepts appear to be separate and unrelated, their impact on understanding leader behaviour is quite significant. Thus, in order to exercise influence over their followers, leaders who are high in personal power need are likely to use their position power base more often – that is, the use of resources such as rights of one's office, ability to exercise coercion, and control over rewards. On the other hand, leaders who are high in the institutional power need are likely to influence their followers more often by the use of their personal power base – that is, the leader expertise or attraction as perceived by the followers.

We now return to the discussion of power motivation and its relation to moral altruism. Individuals high on personal power need are preoccupied with their own interests and concerns. In the organizational context, such self-interest is pursued even at the cost of the organization's welfare and effectiveness. When power is exercised in this manner, the leader demands and expects followers' loyalty and efforts to be directed towards the achievement of the leader's personal goals. For this purpose, the leaders tend to draw on the resources of their position power base. The personal power need of the leader would seem to be rooted in a deep-seated sense of personal insecurity which manifests itself in dictatorial forms of behaviour and defensive feelings in relation with the followers. These leaders, insensitive to the needs of their followers, expect the followers' unquestioning obedience to and compliance with their authority and decisions (Howell and Avolio, 1992).

On the other hand, the dominant preoccupation of individuals high on institutional power need is the interests of the organization and its members. Such individuals subordinate their personal or self-interest to that of the organization, which then becomes the sole reason for their desire to influence and control others. Leaders who are high on institutional power motivation emphasize orderliness, discipline, and task structure primarily to ensure the accomplishment of the organziation's objectives. For this purpose, they draw primarily on the resources of their personal power base – that is, expertise or attraction as perceived by the followers. When they are required to use rewards and sanctions as means of control and influence, they do so impartially and equitably. Contrary to the personal power need, the institutional power need is derived from the leader's identification with and commitment to the organization's objectives and interests. For this reason, power becomes the vehicle to serve the needs of the organization and its members. It is manifested in behaviours and feelings that serve to help and support the followers in accomplishing their tasks. Furthermore, being aware of their need to remedy the inadequacies in their competences and abilities, the institutional power need makes leaders not only establish open communication with their followers, but also create a climate in which followers are encouraged to provide suggestions and criticisms of the leaders' decisions and actions (Howell and Avolio, 1992).

The discussion of the personal power need relative to the institutional power need suggests that personal power need clearly places the interests of self before those of others, and might even be at considerable cost to others; personal power need is the antithesis of altruism. On the other hand, the institutional power need places the interests of others before, and might even be a cost to, self. As McClelland and Burnham (1995) observed, on the basis of their data from stories written by managers:

> the good manager's power motivation is not oriented toward personal aggrandizement but toward the institution he or she serves ... if a high power-motive score is balanced by high inhibition, stories about power tend to be altruistic. That is, the heroes in the story exercise power on behalf of someone else ... as distinguished from the concern for personal power, which is characteristic of individuals whose stories are loaded with power imagery but show no sign of inhibition or self-control. (p. 129)

In a retrospective commentary, twenty years later, McClelland states: 'Indeed, such motivational characteristics continually emerge as what separates world-class managers from mediocre ones' (1995: 139). Since the institutional power need manifests the altruistic motive, we can infer that leaders high on institutional power need are more likely to be effective than those high on personal power need.

The need for achievement, or the achievement motive (McClelland, 1961), is one of the key elements to understand leadership behaviours. Individuals high on the achievement motive derive satisfaction from achieving their goals, as well as from their relentless efforts in pursuit of achievement almost as an end in itself. They assume a high degree of personal responsibility but also tend to be self-oriented in that they view organizational resources and support primarily in terms of their own objectives. Similar to the affiliation and power needs, discussed previously, individuals high on the need for achievement might be motivated either by 'personal achievement' or by 'social achievement' (Mehta, 1994). Leaders driven by personal achievement motives are more likely to engage in behaviours that benefit self rather than others '... because they focus on personal improvement and doing things better by themselves, achievement-motivated people want to do things themselves' (McClelland, 1995: 126).

On the other hand, leaders driven by the social achievement motive show a concern for others and initiate efforts '... in terms of articulation of individual and collective capability, concern for a better quality of life and need to engage in meaningful organizational and social action in order to influence the environment' (Mehta, 1994: 171). Thus, leaders motivated by social achievement would generally tend towards efforts which primarily benefited others. However, leaders motivated by personal achievement could also engage in efforts that benefit others when the objective of their efforts also included the interests of others. For example, when leaders engage in self-development the objective might be viewed as 'personal achievement'. However, if the ultimate objective of the leader is to prepare himself or herself to better serve the followers, then such achievement motivation would be congruent with the altruistic motive. In fact, it is not uncommon for effective charismatic leaders motivated by altruism to pay attention to continuous self-improvement or self-development which enables them to better perform the several behaviours in the leadership process.

To summarize the discussion so far: as indicated in Chapter 3, leadership is both a relational and a followers' attribution phenomenon. Leadership behaviours are identified always in the context of the leader-follower inter-action and never in isolation. Consequently, the motivation underlying lea-der behaviours can be characterized either as altruistic or egotistic. The altruistic motivation of a leader manifests itself at the operative level in terms of affiliative interest, institutional power need, self-discipline or self-development and social achievement needs. The egotistic motivation of a leader, on the other hand, expresses itself in affiliative assurance, personal power need, and personal achievement chiefly in terms of self-aggrandizement. These differences are summarized in Table 4.1.

Table 4.1 Two contrasting leadership motive patterns

Underlying **Motive**	Altruistic [Intent to] [benefit] [others]	Egotistic [Intent to] [benefit] [self]
Operative **Needs**	Affiliative interest Institutional power Social achievement Self-discipline/self-development	Affiliative assurance Personal power Personal achievement Self-aggrandizement
Influence **Strategy**	Empowerment Referent and expert power base	Control Legal, coercive, and reward power base
Leadership **Effectiveness**	High	Low

Source: Kanungo & Mendonca (1996); reprinted with permission

We also see from this table that leaders with an altruistic motivation influence followers through the strategies of empowerment and the use of expertise and attraction to their followers; whereas, leaders with an egotistical motivation influence followers through control strategies and the use of legal coercion, and rewards and sanctions. The leadership influence strategies and processes have been referred to and described in this and in previous chapters, but their ethical or moral implications will be explored in detail in the next section.

In conclusion, we can say that the charismatic leadership role is effective when the leader behaviours are motivated by the altruistic motive. At any given point in time, it is possible for the charismatic leader to be motivated by one or more needs such as the needs for affiliation, power, and achievement. However, regardless of the need that operates as the motive, the leader's effectiveness will ultimately depend upon whether the behaviours manifested by that need are a reflection of and are guided by the overarching altruistic need.

The ethical dimensions of the leadership influence processes

Leadership as a social influence process

In the preceding sections, we focused on an aspect of the leadership phenomenon, as a leader-centred construct; and, therefore, examined the leader's motivational dispositions that trigger and sustain leadership role behaviours. However, the leader's behaviours are designed to influence the followers' values, attitudes, and behaviours. So this aspect of the leader role behaviours provides the basis of another approach to understanding leadership, which is to view it as a social influence process. This approach allows us to explore the psychological underpinnings or explanations of the influence process involved in the leader-follower relationship. The focus on the influence processes highlights the leadership phenomenon as a relational construct. The leader-centred and the relational approaches are, of course, not mutually exclusive, but complementary. Therefore, both approaches become necessary for a sound and proper understanding of leadership.

In the sections that follow, we discuss the leadership influence processes and the related influence strategies. More specifically, we explore the two basic influence processes available to leaders: the transactional influence process and the transformational influence process. The various types of these influence processes have been identified and described in the discussion of the modal orientations in leadership in Chapter 3. The major thrust of the discussion here is to explore the ethical or moral dimensions of the leadership influence processes and related strategies. For this purpose, we shall first examine the nature of the influence processes and related strategies and the underlying psychological mechanics and dynamics through which the beliefs, attitudes, and behaviours of both the followers and leaders are affected.

The transactional influence process

In the transactional influence process, the leader ensures that followers perform the required behaviours and demonstrate commitment and loyalty through the use of rewards and sanctions. The transactional mode of exercising leadership influence is implicit in the major leadership roles of: the people orientation or social role; the task orientation or the task role; and the participative role. What precisely are the psychological dynamics that operate in the transactional influence process? What are the effects of this process on the leader and the followers? What are the ethical or moral implications of such effects?

The psychological mechanisms and dynamics of the transactional influence process can be explained in terms of the theoretical perspectives derived from: the leaders' bases of social power (French and Raven, 1959); the nature of social exchange (Blau, 1974; Hollander, 1979); and the motivational dynamics (Evans, 1970; House, 1971; Luthans and Kreitner, 1975). Implicit in these perspectives is the rationale that leaders have at their command and under their control a host of resources which are valued by followers because these resources are instrumental in satisfying the followers' salient needs. These resources or strategies, described in Chapter 3, can be summarized as: contingent or non-contingent rewards and punishment; authority of office or position; expertise or specialized knowledge, or innovative ideas; actions to facilitate performance; setting goals and providing feedback; opportunities to participate in decision-making; loyalty and commitment to followers.

Consequently, leaders can offer these resources to followers in exchange for the followers' compliance with the leader's demands or directives, as well as for the followers' commitment and loyalty to the leader. As demonstrated by the work of Katz and Kahn (1978), the compliance behaviours can be traced to and explained by reward, coercive and legal power strategies of the leader. The operation of the reward and coercive strategies in inducing follower compliance is understood by the motivational process postulated by expectancy theory (Lawler, 1967; Kanungo and Mendonca, 1997). Thus, followers are motivated to perform the behaviours desired by the leader when followers expect that certain outcomes follow the performance of the behaviours and the followers value these outcomes.

In the reward strategy, the outcomes expected by the followers are the variety of rewards under the leader's control. Since followers value these rewards and will receive them only on performance of the behaviours desired by the leader, the followers are motivated to perform these behaviours. The coercive strategy operates in a similar manner, except that in this case the followers avoid the undesired behaviours. The leader is able to influence followers to desist from undesirable behaviours because followers expect certain sanctions, which they do not value, should they perform these behaviours. The fear of the sanctions then becomes the basis for the influence process. In the legal strategy, followers comply because their socialization – either in terms of the sociocultural context or that of the organization's internal work culture – has prepared them to recognize or perceive that the leader has legitimate authority to require that followers perform certain behaviours. The followers' socialization thus plays a more significant role in the explanation of the social influence process of the legal power strategy.

The key or significant aspect about these resources and strategies – more particularly about the way these are used – is that they enable the leader to develop a *quid pro quo* relationship with their followers. The objective of such a relationship would seem to be nothing more than that the followers should comply with the leader's goals, objectives, and directives. There is clearly no intention or desire on the part of leaders who adopt the transactional influence process to bring about a change in the individuals' attitudes or values or to facilitate the identification with or the internalization of the organization's mission and norms; neither do these leaders seek to promote the growth and development of the followers.

The focus of the transactional influence process is solely on the leader's objectives, needs and concerns. It is, therefore, not surprising if the effectiveness of the transactional influence mode is limited to the motivational 'life-span' of the various commodities or strategies that are used. The transactional influence process has serious ethical and moral implications which we examine from the point of view of the followers, the organization, and the leader. This approach to exercising social influence tends to regard followers, at best, as providers of knowledge, abilities, skills and efforts which the leaders need to accomplish their own objectives. At worst, it views followers as mere instruments or appendages of machines which can be traded so long as the price is right. There is no consideration in the transactional influence process of the followers' needs and aspirations, and of providing them with an opportunity and the means to identify with and internalize the idealized vision formulated by the leader for the organization. Consequently, it offends against the dignity of the human person; it also frustrates the basic human needs of maintaining self-worth and, as a result, causes much psychological and, sometimes, physical harm to employees (Sashkin, 1984).

In organizations where the transactional influence process prevails, followers will soon cease to experience dignity, meaning, and community so essential for the growth of both the organization and its members. In addition, such a process can lead to an inefficient deployment of the organization's resources, for several reasons. First, leaders who use the transactional influence process are more likely to focus on the status quo – that is, to attend to the routine, day-to-day caretaker activities of the organization. Leaders generally find such a focus to be more convenient as it does not require them to exert the effort and experience the insecurity, uncertainty and risks associated with change in the status quo. Nevertheless, the organization and its various stakeholders, including its members and the community in which it operates, are deprived of the benefits which accrue from strategies and actions to remedy the deficiencies in the status quo, and to assess and exploit the opportunities that abound in the environment.

Second, there is the possibility that the transactional influence process can stem from the leader's operative motives of affiliative assurance, personal power, or personal achievement. The ethical implications of behaviours prompted by these motives have been fully discussed in the previous section. It is useful to recognize that such motives of their leaders are readily transparent to the followers. As a result, the message to followers might be that the end justifies the means, and the leaders' behaviours in accord with this principle might serve as a role model and, thereby, lead to similar unethical behaviours by the followers. Even if it does not, they will certainly not be inspired to function in a manner which serves the best interests of the organization. The third reason for the inefficient deployment of organizational resources results from the effects which result when leaders not only do not function as role models for followers but, through the transactional influence process, communicate to followers the message that they either do not have a significant role to play, or that they do not have the capacity to make a meaningful contribution. The organization is, thus, deprived of the enormous resources of its members – their knowledge, skills, abilities, innovative ideas and efforts, commitment and loyalty remain untapped.

When we consider the moral implications of the transactional influence process from the point of view of the leader, we must distinguish two types of motives behind the leader's transactional influence. These are: intention to serve mutual interest of both self and other (mutual altruism); and intention to serve the interest of self alone using the other as the means for this purpose (egotism). The moral justification for mutual altruistic motive of the leader comes from the teleological approach to ethics discussed in Chapter 2. But the egotistic motive of the leader in the transactional influence is not conducive to the development of the organization's moral environment, which is a crucial responsibility of organizational leaders (Kanungo, 2001). Such an approach, as mentioned earlier, could create a climate that breeds dysfunctional norms and values, which lead to conflict rather than cooperation among individuals and between departments because each now place their own interests before those of others without any regard to the superordinate interests of the organization, and to the organization's responsibilities and obligations to its external stakeholders. In the transactional influence mode, the exercise of power, as noted earlier, is primarily to serve the interests of the leader rather than those of the followers. Hence, it has the potential to severely impair the leader's eventual effectiveness because, as Lord Acton observed: 'Power tends to corrupt and absolute power corrupts absolutely' (quoted in Bartlett, 1968: 750a).

The transformational influence process

In the transformational influence process, the leader works to bring about a change in the followers' attitudes and values as he or she moves the organization towards its future goals. In this process, leaders also use resources – including rewards and sanctions at their disposal. But, the use of resources is designed for one sole purpose and that is to influence followers to internalize the goals, beliefs, and values which are inherent in the vision. The transformational mode of exercising leadership influence is very explicit in the charismatic leadership role. However, it is important to recognize that when the leader adopts the charismatic role, he or she does not abandon the social role, the task role and the participative role. These roles are performed by the charismatic leader as and when necessary to realize the vision and consistently with its beliefs and values. What precisely are the psychological dynamics which operate in the transformational influence process? What are the effects of this process on the leaders and the followers? What are the ethical or moral implications of such effects?

In order to understand the psychological mechanisms or dynamics underlying the transformational influence process, we shall draw on the social psychological theories of influence processes (notably the work of Kelman, 1958; French and Raven, 1959), of influence tactics (McClelland, 1975), and of empowerment (Conger and Kanungo, 1988c; Thomas and Velthouse, 1990). However, the basic psychological dynamics which seem to operate in the transformational influence process relate to two factors: (a) the internalization by the followers of the leader's vision; and (b) the enhancement of the followers' self-efficacy belief – that is, the belief that they are capable of working to realize the goals of the vision. The followers' compliance behaviours, their commitment and loyalty to the leader, stem from these two factors. The change in the followers' attitudes and values, therefore, results essentially from the leader's empowerment of the followers.

Although the several social psychological theories of influence processes and tactics help us to understand the transformational influence effects in leadership, the leaders' empowerment strategies and the resulting empowering experience of followers seem to be critical ingredients to the success of the transformational influence process. As will be seen from the sections that follow, it is implicit and, in fact, inherent to the charismatic leadership process described in Chapter 3. It will be recalled from that description that the charismatic leadership process consists of three stages, with a set of beha-viours in each stage. The three stages are: (1) evaluation of the status quo; (2) formulation of organizational goals; and (3) the means to achieve. We shall consider how the transformational influence process is carried out through the activities in each stage.

In the first stage, the critical leader behaviours are the assessment of the environment, which includes a careful and thorough analysis of the available resources, opportunities and constraints, and of followers' needs and aspira-tions. It also includes recognition of the deficiencies in the status quo, par-ticularly in the context of the available opportunities and of followers' needs. The information gathered from such an environmental assessment becomes the foundation for leader activities and behaviours in the next stage of the charismatic leadership process. However, it is important to recognize that right from the beginning the leader's focus is not on his or her own self or interests, but on others – the interests, needs, and aspirations of the orga-nization and its members, the deficiencies in the status quo which impedes the fulfilment of these needs and the realization of these interests and as-pirations. This focus on the 'other' rather than on 'self', is a significant, if not the key, element in preparing a climate which is conducive to change in the followers' attitudes and values.

Following upon the first stage, the predominant activity and behaviour in the second stage relates to the formulation and articulation of the vision. Motivated by the desire to remedy the deficiencies in the status quo and to seize upon the opportunities which would benefit the organization and its members, the leader formulates a vision that has three important character-istics: it is *discrepant* from the status quo, *idealized*, and *shared* by the followers. Critical to the effectiveness of the transformational influence process is an idealized and shared vision. When leaders formulate an idealized vision which represents a state of profound consciousness, the leaders are enabled to identify with and commit themselves to achieve the vision. This process of leader's identification and commitment, and the exertion of efforts to realize the vision, directly contributes to the leader's self-development and self-ac-tualization. Such self-transformation of the leader then becomes the model that inspires the followers to undergo a similar inner transformation.

It is necessary to recognize that the charismatic leader's self-transformation, which triggers the transformational influence process, is more than the satisfaction of the leader's need for achievement. It has a spiritual quality which transcends the mere mundane or material sense of self-development in terms of the acquisition of some skills or attainment of an objective. The analysis of self-identity in terms of Roland's (1988) con-ceptualization of self may be used here to further emphasize the point that the self-transformation of charismatic leaders has indeed a spiritual compo-nent. Roland (1988) suggests that self-identify can be described as the basic inner psychological organization that enables us to develop internalized world views. Since the inner psychological organizations differ from person to person, our self-identities, along with our internalized world views, differ, resulting in the profound differences in meaning we attach to our everyday experiences and relationships. Roland (1988) asserts that there are three types of 'overarching or superordinate organizations of the self: the familial self, the individualized self, and the spiritual self' (p. 6). Each individual has the potential to develop self-identity along each of these dimensions of human experience.

The individualized self is characterized by an emphasis on the self-contained, competitive, individualistic 'I-ness', autonomous functioning, inner separateness, contractual and egalitarian relationships. This is the predominant mode of self-identity in North American societies. The familial self is characterized by 'symbiosis-reciprocity' that involves collectivistic orientation, a sense of 'we-ness', emotional intimacy with the in-group members, interdependence and reciprocal relationships. This is the predominant mode of self-identity in Eastern societies such as India, China, and Japan. The individualized and the familial selves are similar to the constructs of individualism-collectivism suggested by Hofstede (1980) and Triandis (1988). The third type of self that Roland postulates is the spiritual self. The spiritual self is characterized by a realization of inner virtues and strengths, the spiritual reality or the ideals which the self tries to attain. For a person with a spiritual self-identity, 'the fundamental goal of all relationships and living is the gradual self-transformation toward finer and subtler qualities and refined aspects of power in the quest for self-realization' (Roland, 1988: 294).

This mode of self-identity is often observed in Eastern societies such as India and Japan, but is somewhat rare in the North American context. In the highly individualistic culture of North America, the existence of the spiritual dimension of human experience is often ignored or treated reductively as an aberration of the normal experience of the mundane. And yet, the spiritual self-identity is precisely what characterizes the inner psychological world views of the charismatic leaders. Their identification and commitment to idealized values, their efforts to develop finer and subtler qualities in themselves, their own inner self-transformation and their missionary zeal to bring about similar transformation in others are all reflections of their spiritual self-identity. Of course, the charismatic leaders' missionary zeal needs to be distinguished from that of the irrational, fanatical zealots who stop at nothing to thrust their views and ideals upon their followers. The distinction is that the charismatic leaders' vision is *shared* by the followers and it is for this reason that the transformational influence process ensures that charismatic leadership is more enduring and more effective.

The articulation of the vision is an equally important behavioural component of the second stage. The formulation of the vision, although critical, remains an academic exercise unless it is communicated to the followers. As stated earlier, the contents of the vision are: the nature of the status quo and its shortcomings, the beneficial opportunities that exist, and how the status quo prevents the organization and its members from availing of these opportunities; the nature of the vision and how, when realized, it will remedy the existing deficiencies and become the most effective vehicle to bring about the fulfilment of the hopes of the followers; and, finally, the plan of action which provides the broad framework of strategies that are necessary to translate the vision into reality. The mode of communication is as important as the contents of the vision. Hence, the need for effective articulation.

However, the articulation of the vision must convey the central idea that the vision is more than a 'Pisgah' view of the future – that it is an attainable goal. Articulation, thus, becomes the expression of the most profound convictions and beliefs of the leader. The communication of these convictions and beliefs, in practical terms, means that the leader evokes in followers the same passion and zeal that the leader has for the vision. For this purpose, the articulation of the vision will emphasize the attainability of the vision and, more importantly, the leader's convictions that the followers have the capability, resources, and the courage to do what is necessary to attain the vision. In this process, leaders will also draw attention to their own expertise which testifies to their capability, and their willingness, to work with and support their followers' efforts.

The effects of the leaders' formulation and articulation of the vision, as just described, is to engender in followers trust in the leader. The followers' trust is earned not just by inspirational articulation of the vision, although this is necessary. It is not developed by the statement of the vision and of the leaders' expertise in glowing and convincing terms, although this is also necessary. The followers begin to trust their leader when they perceive, beyond a shadow of doubt, that their leader is unflinchingly dedicated to the vision and is willing to work towards it even at the risk of considerable personal cost and sacrifice. Although the first two stages of the charismatic leadership process explain the psychological dynamics of the transformational influence process, it is really the third stage – that is, the actual activities and behaviours to achieve the vision – which provides a complete understanding of the effectiveness of the transformational influence process. The charismatic leader activities and behaviours in this stage that are the crux of the transformational influence process are: (a) the empowerment strategies; (b) the strategy relating to outcomes or opportunities provided to followers; and (c) the mode of exercising leadership power. We examine each of these in some detail.

The empowerment strategies

In the fields of industrial sociology and organizational behaviour, most theorists have dealt with 'empowerment' as a set of managerial techniques without paying sufficient attention to the nature and processes underlying the construct. This may have created a management ethos regarding some techniques to overcome worker alienation, but this focus has not adequately increased our understanding of the notion of empowerment and the theoretical and moral rationale for related delineation practices. For example, until the work of Conger and Kanungo (1988c), most scholars assumed that empowerment is the same as managers delegating or sharing power with subordinates. Viewing this traditional approach to empowerment as too limiting, Conger and Kanungo (1988c) have argued for an alternate interpretation and have identified a number of contexts most appropriate for empowerment practices within organizations. The following section briefly describes the analysis of Conger and Kanungo of the empowerment process. Their analysis demonstrates that empowerment strategies are at the core of the transformational influence leadership process.

Conger and Kanungo (1988c) proposed that empowerment can be viewed in two different ways: as a relational and as a motivational construct. If one considers empowerment as a relational construct, then one must understand it in terms of the relational dynamics of power sharing among workers and management. Thus, empowerment becomes the process by which management gives away or shares power with workers. Power, in this context, is interpreted as the possession of formal authority or control over organizational resources. The emphasis is primarily on the notion of sharing authority and resources. Burke's (1986) position is representative in this regard: 'To empower, implies the granting of power – delegation of authority' (p. 51). The Merriam Webster's Dictionary similarly describes the verb 'to empower' as 'to authorize or delegate or give legal power to someone'. In the organizational literature, this idea of delegation and the decentralization of decision-making power is central to the empowerment notion (Kanter, 1983; Burke, 1986).

As a result, management practitioners equate empowerment with participative management techniques such as management by objectives (MBO), quality circles, and goal setting by subordinates as the means of sharing power or delegating authority (McGregor, 1960; Likert, 1961, 1967). However, this line of reasoning does not adequately address the nature of empowerment as experienced by workers because: (a) it assumes that these are the only techniques which will automatically empower the workers; (b) it does not explore the psychological mechanisms underlying empowerment; (c) the effects of these techniques are assumed to be the same as the effects of an empowering experience; and (d) it does not consider the moral justification for these techniques, nor does it consider whether the conflict and tension which might be generated by the techniques are morally defensible.

The second way of interpreting empowerment as a motivational construct stems from the social psychological literature. Here, empowerment is used as a motivational and/or expectancy belief state internal to individuals. For instance, individuals are assumed to have a need for power (McClelland, 1975) where power connotes an internal urge to influence and control other people. A related but more inclusive disposition to control and cope with life events has also been proposed by several psychologists while dealing with the issues of primary/secondary control (Rothbaum, Weisz, and Snyder, 1982), internal/external locus of control (Rotter, 1966), and learned helplessness (Abramson, Garber, and Seligman, 1980). Individuals feel empowered when they perceive that they can adequately cope with events, situations, and/or the people they confront. On the other hand, individuals feel powerless when they believe that they are unable to cope with the physical and social demands of the environment.

Empowerment in this motivational sense also refers to a belief in self-determination (Deci, 1975) or a belief in personal self-efficacy (Bandura, 1986) as the individual copes with environmental demands. Any organizational strategy or technique that strengthens this self-determination or self-efficacy belief of workers will tend to make them feel empowered at work and, consequently, de-alienated. Conversely, any strategy that weakens their self-determination or efficacy belief will increase their sense of personal powerlessness or alienation in relation to the work context. In fact, the Concise Oxford English Dictionary (1964) defines the verb 'empower' as 'to enable'. In contrast to the earlier definition of empowerment as 'delegation' (of authority and resource sharing), the connotation of 'enabling' implies motivation through the enhancement of one's personal efficacy and ability to cope with environmental demands.

In view of the conceptual difficulties raised in connection with empowerment as a relational construct, Conger and Kanungo (1988c) proposed that empowerment be viewed as a motivational construct – meaning 'to enable' rather than simply 'to delegate'. Enabling implies the creation of conditions which heighten the motivation for task accomplishment through the development of a strong sense of personal efficacy. The moral justification for empowerment strategies lies in viewing empowerment as an enabling, rather than as a delegating, process. Alienation, or a sense of powerlessness, cripples the workers by 'disabling' them; empowerment, or an enhancement of self-efficacy, develops workers by 'enabling' them. Managerial practices that cripple workers' potential are morally wrong, but empowerment practices that develop workers' potential are ethical imperatives – more fully discussed in a later section.

Empowerment as a de-alienating strategy becomes critical when subordinates feel powerless and self-estranged. Thus, it is important to identify conditions within organizations (structures and processes) that foster these variants of alienation among subordinates. Once the antecedent conditions of alienation are identified, empowerment strategies and interventions can then be utilized to remove these conditions or to minimize their 'disabling' effects (Kanungo, 1992; Kanungo and Mendonca, 1995). However, just the removal of external conditions (through restructuring, altering policies, re-designing jobs, and so on) is neither always possible nor sufficient to result in the workers experiencing empowerment, unless the strategies and interventions directly provide them with information that enhances their personal efficacy. Bandura (1986) suggests several sources from which individuals directly receive information about their personal efficacy. These sources are good guides for developing the appropriate empowerment strategies.

Conger and Kanungo (1988c) have proposed a five-stage model of the empowerment process that might help leaders develop effective empowerment strategies. The first stage is the diagnosis of conditions within the organization which is responsible for the feelings of the powerlessness and types of alienation among organizational members and attempts to reduce or eliminate them. An extensive list of such contextual conditions has been prepared by Conger and Kanungo (1988c) as a diagnostic checklist. Such a diagnosis prepares leaders for stage two, which is the use of empowerment strategies such as participative management, goal setting, modelling, and so on. The employment of these strategies is aimed at not only removing some of the external conditions responsible for alienation but, more importantly, at providing followers with the self-efficacy information which is discussed in stage three.

A number of leadership practices can be identified that can heighten a sense of self-efficacy among followers. At an interpersonal level, leaders should express confidence in followers accompanied by high performance expectations (Burke, 1986; Neilsen, 1986; House, 1988b), encourage participation in decision-making (Strauss, 1977; Kanter, 1979; Burke, 1986; Neilsen, 1986; Block, 1987; House, 1988b), provide autonomy from bureaucratic constraint (Kanter, 1979; Block, 1987; House, 1988b) and set inspirational and/or meaningful goals (McClelland, 1975; Burke, 1986; Tichy and De-vanna, 1986; Block, 1987; Conger and Kanungo, 1987).

In order to be effective, the empowerment practices outlined above must also directly provide information to followers about their personal efficacy, as required by stage three of the model. Bandura (1986) identified four sources of such information: enactive attainment, vicarious experience, verbal persuasion, and emotional arousal state. Information in personal efficacy through enactive attainment refers to an individual's authentic mastery experience directly related to the job. When followers perform complex tasks or are given more responsibility in their jobs, participate in goal setting, decision-making, and so on, they have the opportunity to test their efficacy.

Sashkin (1984) has advocated participation in four areas such as setting goals, making decisions, solving problems, and making changes in organizations as ethical imperatives. The reasons for Sashkin's advocacy lie not in the opportunity for participation *per se*, but rather in the personal efficacy information that such participation provides through enactive attainment. Participation in goal setting increases the followers' goal acceptance and commitment (Locke and Latham, 1984) because it increases the followers' understanding of what their tasks are and how to go about accomplishing the tasks and, as a result, their confidence in their ability to attain the goal. Any kind of initial success experience in handling tasks, and various training experiences in acquiring new skills, can make the followers feel more capable and, therefore, empowered.

The feeling of being empowered can also come from vicarious experiences of observing others perform successfully on the job. Such modelling techniques can often be used to empower followers. Very often the leader's exemplary behaviours empower followers to believe that they can behave in a like manner, or at least can achieve some improvement in their performance (Conger and Kanungo, 1987). Words of encouragement, verbal feedback, and other forms of social persuasion can be used by leaders to empower followers and by followers to empower their peers. Finally, the personal competence expectations are affected by the emotional arousal state of the individual. Empowerment techniques and strategies that reduce stress and provide emotional support to followers and that create a supportive and trusting group atmosphere (Neilsen, 1986) can be more effective in strengthening self-efficacy beliefs.

The final two stages of the empowerment process suggested by Conger and Kanungo (1988c) describe the nature of empowering experience and its behavioural effects. As a result of receiving self-efficacy information from the leadership practices outlined above, followers feel empowered, that is, the belief in their own capabilities is strengthened, or the belief in their powerlessness is weakened. The behavioural effects of empowerment as a de-alienating experience results in followers both initiating and persevering in work behaviour, and thereby makes the quality of their life at work more rich, active and dynamic. As Bandura (1977) points out, 'The strength of peoples' conviction in their own effectiveness is likely to affect whether they would even try to cope with given situations ... they get involved in activities and behave assuredly when they judge themselves capable of handling situations that would otherwise be intimidating ... efficacy expectations determine how much effort people will expend and how long they will persist in the face of obstacles and aversive experiences' (pp. 193–4). Self-assured followers tend to be more satisfied, more productive, and contribute more to organization and the society at large. In a recent study (Conger, Kanungo, and Menon, 2000), it was found that charismatic leadership behaviour leads to not only a sense of collective identity and perceived group task performance, but also to feelings of empowerment among followers.

Strategy relating to outcomes and opportunities

The empowerment strategy should flow naturally from an organizational culture and philosophy that is congruent with values and norms that are consistent with and support the empowerment of followers. These values and norms are: self-determination, collaboration rather than conflict or competition, high performance standards and expectations, non-discrimination, and meritocracy (House, 1988a). For this purpose, the reward systems should be designed to emphasize innovative performance as well as high performance levels. Critical to the reward system design is that the rewards are valued by followers and are contingent on task performance and related behaviours, which followers see are appropriate and conducive to the realization of the established vision and goals (Kanter, 1979; Kanungo, 1987). Furthermore, the design and administration of the reward system is conducted in a fair and equitable manner.

When leaders are not concerned with or are indifferent to procedural justice, when they do not administer rewards fairly but in an arbitrary or capricious way, as is often the case when leaders are influenced by the ingratiating behaviours of some followers, then followers experience dissatisfaction with leaders' decisions. Such decisions suggest a rather patronizing attitude of the leader towards the followers. The uncertainty and inequity of outcomes which result from the leaders' patronizing attitude and behaviours leads to several undesirable consequences. It reduces the followers' beliefs that their efforts to realize the vision will lead to the expected beneficial outcomes. It causes the leaders to lose credibility in the eyes of the followers, which adversely affects followers' trust and confidence in the vision. Finally, it reduces the followers' motivation to exert the required effort towards the attainment of the vision.

The empowerment of followers is also greatly enhanced when leaders exercise the expert and referent power strategies (French and Raven, 1959). In these strategies, the source of the transformational influence is not the organization, but the leaders themselves. The leaders' expert power is effective in the influence process because followers perceive their leaders to possess the knowledge, abilities, and expertise which followers can draw upon and which they see to be necessary for the attainment of the vision. The followers' perception that their leader possesses the needed expertise makes the leader credible and trustworthy. Similar to the expert power, the leaders' referent power also lies in the followers' perceptions of the leaders' commitment to their welfare. In this case too, it is not enough that leaders have certain personal qualities and characteristics – however noble or endearing these might be. The leaders' influence on followers is derived from the fact that followers perceive the leaders' efforts to be selfless and their intent to be altruistic. As a result of such perceptions, the followers are attracted to and identify with the leaders.

Although the strategies relating to outcomes and opportunities have been discussed separately from the empowerment strategies, their effects on the followers are the same – that is, all these strategies contribute to transforming the self-efficacy beliefs of the followers. Through these strategies, followers are 'enabled' to perform well beyond the organization's expectations (Bass, 1985). The preceding discussion explored the nature of the psychological dynamics which explain the transformational influence processes of leadership. We conclude with an examination of the processes of attitudinal change proposed by Kelman (1958). His formulation provides a fuller understanding of the psychological dynamics at work in both the transactional and transformational influence processes of leadership. It also provides a base from which to examine the moral or ethical dimensions of leadership influence processes.

According to Kelman (1958), there are three processes of attitude change: compliance, identification, internalization. Thus: in compliance: '. . . an individual accepts influence . . . adopts the induced behavior – not because he believes in its content – but because he expects to gain specific rewards or approval and avoid specific punishments or disapproval by conforming' (Kelman, 1958: 53). The followers' compliance behaviour depends on the leaders' control on rewards and punishment and, further, on the leaders' continuous monitoring of the followers' behaviour. The change in the followers is temporary and superficial. It does not extend to change in the followers' attitudes, beliefs and values. As indicated previously, it is typical of the transactional influence process of leadership.

The next change relates to identification which occurs when '. . . an individual accepts influence because he wants to establish or maintain a satisfying self-defining relationship to another person . . . The individual actually believes in the responses which he adopts through identification, but their specific content is more or less irrelevant' (Kelman, 1958: 53). The followers are attracted to the leader 'as a person' – the leader's qualities, characteristics, reputation, and so on which might be analogous to 'hero-worship'. But, it is important to note that the attraction is not based on the leader's control over rewards and sanctions. Of course, the leader's influence will operate so long as the attraction of the followers continues. In the internalization process of attitude change, the '. . . individual accepts influence because of the content of the induced behavior – the ideas and actions of which it is composed – is intrinsically rewarding . . . because it is congruent with his value system' (Kelman, 1958: 53). In the context of the leader-follower interaction, the leader's vision, values and goals will be the key ingredients in the leadership influence process, provided that followers subscribe to the leader's vision and values and adopt the related norms.

The identification and internalization processes of attitude change help us to understand the nature and success of the transformational influence processes of leadership. These processes also underscore the significance and role of empowerment and related strategies in the transformational influence processes of leadership. The focus of these strategies is on the followers rather than on the leader, and followers clearly understand that the thrust of the leader's message is: 'I will attend to your personal growth and competence regardless of my personal cost and sacrifice'.

The ethical implications of the transactional and transformational influence processes

The preceding discussion clearly demonstrates that leadership effectiveness is greater and more enduring when leaders adopt the transformational influence process mode. The means used for this purpose, empowerment and related strategies, reflect the altruistic value and orientation. In contrast, the nature of the control strategy adopted in the transactional influence processes is manipulative and reflects an egotistical value orientation, because it is primarily intended to benefit 'self' even at the cost of the 'other'. We have seen that the empowerment strategies proposed by Conger and Kanungo (1988c) are at the core of effective transformational influence processes. These strategies, by their very nature, involve a concern for 'other before self' which must be manifested at every stage of the charismatic leadership process – from the assessment of the environment, formulation and articulation of the vision, to the means to achieve the vision.

In Chapter 2, we explored the basis of moral altruism. This value becomes even more crucial and pivotal when we discuss the transformational influence process which directly involves the relationship between persons. The empowerment and related strategies are an ideal way for leaders to exercise ethically the social influence process of leadership. However, is there an ethical imperative for leaders to empower their followers for reasons which go well beyond the pragmatic considerations of the 'bottom line'? In other words, do leaders have the moral obligation to empower their followers and, thereby, promote their growth and development even if such development means that they might leave the organization to join its competitors? This is a pertinent question, particularly in the context of work organizations where managers seek to adopt the charismatic leadership role in relation to their subordinates. To address this question, one needs to explore the human value and morality of work.

In such an exploration, one cannot escape the realization that work is inextricably bound up with human existence. To a human being, work is more than a means of earning one's livelihood. It is an essential means of self-development and of the development of society, its science, technology, and culture. It is a free, conscious act of a human being and, as a consequence, work acquires its value from the dignity of the human being as a person. Work, its content and context, should, therefore, promote rather than damage the dignity of the human being. This vision of the values of human work is often blurred, if not gravely distorted, when work is viewed in terms of social exchange theory, as a commodity which is sold by the employee in return for wages and benefits; and the employer, by virtue of his/her ownership of capital, assumes the right to regard employees as instruments in the production process. Such a view distorts the reality because even though the worker does not own the capital (technology, know-how, and so on) it is the worker who uses or operates it. Therefore, in the production process, the worker is the primary efficient cause, while capital remains a mere instrument in the hands of the workers. Furthermore, the right to private property (including the right to capital) is not an absolute right. It is subject to the right which every human being has to access and use the resources of nature – the common patrimony of humanity. From this standpoint, capital is the result of the interaction (direct or indirect) between the owner's labours and the natural resources. Therefore, when workers are engaged in the production process, they are entitled to consider themselves as part-owners of the capital that is employed.

These truths, so evident from mankind's historical experience, confirm the principle of the priority of labour over capital, which is acquired through work in order that it may serve work in the future. Certain specific rights flow from this principle, rights that go beyond the right to proper working conditions and remuneration. These rights include work whose content and context (including the superior-subordinate relationship) do not treat employees as instruments of production, but accord to them their due rights as a primary efficient cause of production, with the right and duty to take such initiatives as one would if one were self-employed. In other words, the organization must also enable its employees to preserve their awareness that they are working for themselves, an approach that alone is consistent with the dignity of the human person. As the Second Vatican Council declared: 'Just as human activity proceeds from man, so it is ordered towards man. For when a man works he not only alters things and society, he develops himself as well. He learns much, he cultivates his resources, he goes outside of himself and beyond himself . . . rightly understood, this kind of growth is of greater value than any external riches which can be garnered' (1966: 233).

In addition to the employee rights which impose moral obligations upon the manager, there are also the obligations which spring from the fact that the manager is a member of the work community and is expected to exercise a leadership role in the community. In the words of Pope John-Paul II, '. . . work bears a particular mark of man and of humanity, the mark of a person operating within a community of persons' (1981: 4). The manager and his/her subordinates constitute one such community in a work organization. It seems clearly evident that the human value and morality of work creates an obligation for the manager to be responsible for the development of the members of his/her work community. Such a manager clearly has an organic, rather than an atomistic, world view, and moral altruistic motive. The ethical justification of this type of transformational leader is derived from deontological and personalist perspectives, as discussed in Chapter 2.

Does this moral obligation exist even when it is likely that the employee might leave the organization and join the competitor? One might be tempted to respond to this question in the affirmative because the organization might still benefit from good public relations – the very high probability that the people who were treated with dignity would tend to speak well of the organization. However, the response to this question ought to be based on an examination of the basis of the obligation. The preceding discussion makes clear that the obligation does not stem from the pragmatic considerations of the bottom line or similar organizational interests. Rather, it flows from the consideration of human value and morality of work which, unlike the social exchange theory, does not regard employees as mere instruments in the production process. Hence, the only morally defensible limitation on this obligation would be the subordinate's capabilities and willingness to grow and develop in the job.

In the preceding sections, the discussion established that moral altruism is the ideal foundation for ethical leadership. However, some have argued that mutual altruism can also be a basis for ethical leadership. In the following section, we address this issue by comparing the values and beliefs associated with transactional (mutual altruism) and transformational (moral altruism) leadership.

Values and assumptions of transactional and transformational leadership

Table 4.2 summarizes the distinction between the moral foundations of transactional and transformational leadership based on the leaders' motives, values, and assumptions.

On the basis of the influence processes, leaders can be classified as transactional and transformational. Based on their motives and their beliefs, the transactional leaders are of two types: egotistic transactional and mutual altruistic transactional. The egotistic transactional leaders' motives are purely self-serving; whereas the mutual altruistic transactional leaders' motives are directed to serving the interest of self as well as the others in the exchange relationship. They also differ on beliefs regarding their rights and obligations: the egotistic transactional leaders believe that they should act only to protect their self-interest; the mutual altruistic transactional leaders believe that their actions should protect the rights of every individual in the exchange relationship.

Table 4.2 Motives, values and assumptions of leaders

	Transactional Leadership	**Transformational Leadership**
Motive/Intent	Mutual Altruism	Moral Altruism
Internalized norm	Reciprocity norm internalized	Social responsibility norm internalized
Self cognitions	Idiocentric 'Me' self (individualistic) Self Centric	Allocentric 'We' self (embedded self) Socio Centric
Relations to others	Atomistic (independent)	Organic (interdependent)
Rights and obligations	Actions to protect individual rights are valued	Actions that meet social obligations are valued
Nature of goals	Pragmatic goals	Idealistic goals
Evaluation of means and ends	Ends justify means (outcome or teleological orientation)	Both ends and means are justified (process or deontological orientation)
Behavioural strategy to influence others	Utilitarianism: social contract and exchange of resources as basis for influence	Altruism: cultivating personal virtues and empowerment of others as basis of influence
Nature of ethics	Teleological and situational ethics: emphasis on purpose and on particulars	Deontological and principle governed ethics: emphasis on duty and on universals

Source: Kanungo (2001)

Leaders develop these motives and beliefs as a result of their past experience, training, and other forms of socialization. Through socialization practices in family, educational, religious, and other institutions, leaders acquire motives and associated self-cognitions or self-concepts. Internalized ethical norms (or values) resulting from socializations are a part of leaders' self-cognitions. There are two types of ethical norms associated with altruistic motives: the norm of reciprocity and the norm of social responsibility. The reciprocity norm dictates that we do good to others who do good to us (Gouldner, 1960). The reciprocity norm forms the basis of the utilitarian altruism motive and the resource exchange strategy of the mutual altruistic transactional leader. The norm of social responsibility refers to an internalized belief of a moral obligation to help others without any consideration of an expected personal benefit (Berkowitz, 1972; Schwartz, 1975). The social responsibility norm forms the basis of the moral altruism motive and the empowering strategy of the transformational leader. Clearly, the reciprocity and social responsibility norms are used respectively in teleological and deontological ethics for judging the moral status of the leader's motives, strategies, actions and their outcomes.

Triandis (1994) has differentiated between two types of self-concepts, *allocentric* and *idiocentric*, that can result from past socialization. The transformational leader tends to be more allocentric and the transactional leader tends to be more idiocentric. The transformational leader is allocentric because he/she defines self in terms of relating to others, and considers group goals, group achievement, cooperation, endurance, and self-control to be more important. An allocentric transformational leader has a 'we' self-identity. The self is viewed as an extended or embedded self, by identifying it as linked to a collectivity (family, community, organization, nation). The idiocentric transactional leader, on the other hand, defines self as an independent entity, the 'I' or 'me' self, clearly separated from other individuals. The idiocentric self-orientation of the leader is primarily concerned with protecting his/her personal interests as an individual (self-centric), whereas the allocentric self-orientation of the leader is mainly concerned with protecting the interests of the group, knowing that his/her own interests and the group interests are inseparable (socio-centric).

While relating to other people, the idiocentric transactional leader considers the self to be *atomistic* or separate from others, whereas the allocentric transformational leader considers the self as *organic*, or inseparable from others. With the atomistic view of self, the transactional leader puts high value on personal independence (or complete autonomy) and protection of individual rights. On the other hand, with the organic view of self, the transformational leader puts more value on interdependence, conditional autonomy and meeting social obligations towards others. With an atomistic view of self, the transactional leader considers people's relationships to each other in organizations to be contractual in nature. For such a leader, social and legal contracts form the basis of social interactions and exchange of resources among people. The leader's and the followers' personal goals and outcomes are achieved though social contract. A mutually beneficial contract, as opposed to a contract that benefits only one member in the exchange relationship, is considered ethical. The principle of utilitarianism or teleological ethics (an act is ethical if it promotes the greatest happiness of the greatest number), as advocated by Mill (1967), provides the moral justification for the mutually beneficial contracts that transactional leaders value. An allocentric transformational leader with an organic view of the self considers obligatory activities towards others as ideal forms of action or as a moral duty to achieve the common good. Thus, the nature of goals that a leader strives for are viewed as idealistic by the transformational leader, whereas they tend to be viewed as purely pragmatic by the transactional leader.

The above discussion with respect to the assumptions about the nature of goals of a leader implies that for the idiocentric transactional leader the means and ends reflected in actions are judged with an *outcome* or a *teleological orientation*. Such a leader believes that ends justify means. 'All is well that ends well' becomes the motto of the transactional leader. If the social contract ends in mutually beneficial results, then the means the leader has used are morally justified. The transformational leader, on the other hand, considers social obligations as his/her moral duty because they serve the higher purpose of benefiting relevant others (the group or organization from which the leader is inseparable) without any calculation of personal gain in return. This represents a *deontological orientation* that considers actions to be morally right when they stem from a sense of duty or obligation towards others. The transactional leader deals with other people simply as a means to achieve personal goals through the transaction of valued resources, whereas the transformational leader considers other people as ends in themselves and therefore attempts to transform their values, attitudes, and behaviour using empowering influence strategies. The foregoing is consistent with Kant's categorical imperative (Bowie, 1998), and the personalist philosophy discussed in Chapter 2. As pointed out earlier, the interests or motives of the transactional idiocentric leader are self-centric, and the intents of the transformational allocentric leader are socio-centric. The associated ethical behavioural strategy to influence others is to frame the social contract, and to exchange resources in social interactions in the case of transactional leadership. This strategy is a manifestation of utilitarian or mutual altruism. In the case of transformational, leadership, the behavioural influence strategy is to empower others by modelling, or exemplary behaviour (Conger and Kanungo, 1998). This strategy is a manifestation of moral altruism.

Finally, the transactional leaders' emphasis on utilitarianism and reciprocity norms as the basic criteria for judging the ethical nature of leadership behaviour leads them to focus on specific particulars of the leader-follower exchange situation. For a transactional leader, there are no universal invariant principles, policies, or goals applicable to all situations and at all times. The particulars of each situation have to be judged to determine the level of morality by examining the utility maximization achieved for both the leader and the followers. By contrast, transformational leaders always search for invariant universal values or principles to guide their formulation of the ideal vision for the organization. The leader's transformational influence strategy (through empowerment) is then guided by an ethic of duty. Universal principles and a deontological ethic provide stability of behaviour and reflect the personal integrity of the transformational leader across varied situations and across time.

To sum up, a transactional leader is more likely to use situational and teleological ethics, whereas a transformational leader is more inclined to use ethics derived from the deontological and personalist perspectives.

Leader's moral character formation

> For more than five hours, US Senator Jean Carnahan sat patiently as Jeffrey Skilling insisted he knew nothing about the rot that had infected Enron Corp; and then he said: 'There is no time ... where I have asked anyone to compromise their integrity. It just doesn't happen'. Ms. Carnahan had clearly heard enough. 'The bankruptcy of this company does not compare with the bankruptcy of character in the executive suite', she blurted out.
>
> (McKenna, 2002; B8)

> Wangari Mathai, Nobel Peace Prize, 2004, in response to a question on the three most important tasks facing Kenya, observed ' ... we need to promote human development – formation in virtue. Education alone is not enough. There is need for people who are well-rounded, properly formed ... people who understand that their human condition makes them trustees of creation and not owners.'
>
> (Gould, 2005: 2)

These quotes highlight the fundamental importance of character formation. The preceding sections highlight the need for altruistic intent and the transformational mode of influence in ethical leadership. It is not enough for leaders to have the intellectual capacity to distinguish between morally good or evil acts. Leaders must make the effort to habitually incorporate moral principles in their beliefs, values and behaviour. In other words, the leader's character is of paramount importance for two reasons. First, the leader's motives and acts, including influence strategies, are the fruits of the leader's character. Second, the leader is a role model to the followers in respect of both task performance and ethical behaviour. Undeniably, the leader is indeed the soul of the organization; and the leader's beliefs, values and behaviours influence and shape, for better or worse, the organization's moral environment, and has all-encompassing serious ramifications both within and outside the organization.

Ethical leadership is essentially transformational in nature; and includes the self-transformation of both leaders and followers. What can leaders do to prepare themselves and their organizations to meet the challenging demands of ethical imperatives? This question, related to the leader's moral character formation, is discussed in the next chapter.

Suggested questions for reflection

- What are the reasons for leadership effectiveness when the leader performs the behaviours in the three stages of the Conger-Kanungo Charismatic Leadership Model with an altruistic intent?
- What are the reasons for leadership effectiveness when the leader adopts the transformational mode of exercising leadership influence?
- Why is the use of empowerment and related strategies in the third stage of the charismatic leadership process crucial to the effectiveness of the transformational influence process?
- In what way do the values and assumptions of transactional leadership differ from the values and assumptions of transformational leadership?

5 Preparing for ethical leadership in organizations

Synopsis

What can leaders do to prepare themselves and their organizations to meet the challenging demands of ethical leadership? We explore this question in the context of: (1) the existence of formidable obstacles to moral altruism in organizations; and (2) as human systems, organizations must be responsive to human needs in the internal and external environment. To exercise ethical leadership in this context, leaders need to draw upon their inner spiritual strength. For this reason, we explore: the nature of spirituality and its manifestation in the cognitive, affective, and moral character of the individual; and the nature of charismatic leadership in the context of the spiritual experiences of both the leader and the followers when its practice is consistent with moral principles. We conclude with some observations on the sources of spiritual strength, solace, and inspiration which spiritual sages of all time recommend; and which leaders can draw on to exercise leadership that is uplifting both to themselves and to their followers.

Introduction

The practice of ethical leadership is indeed the challenge for organizational leaders in the twenty-first century. As President Mikhail Gorbachev observed in an interview,

> The problem of leadership is of urgent importance. Wherever I go ... people talk about this vacuum in leadership ... I have always tried to bring together and link morality and politics ... The core values – what I call the universal human values of morality – are well known. They have been there since ancient times. Policies that are not anchored in them are ultimately bound to fail, as we have seen time and again, including recently in my own country.
>
> (Puffer, 1999: 14)

Clearly, charismatic leadership needs great inner strength to meet the challenging demands of the role. The question we now address is: How do managers prepare themselves for the charismatic leadership role? The sections that follow explore this question from the point of view of two different but related aspects. First, the need to recognize that the sociocultural environment in which leaders function might not be particularly conducive or receptive to altruistic behaviour. For this reason, we examine the obstacles to altruism in the organizational context. Second, we discuss some of the sources that charismatic leaders might draw upon to develop as moral people possessed of inner strength and resourcefulness, and to develop the moral environment of the organization in order to ensure that its culture might be imbued with the spirit of altruism.

Obstacles to altruism in organizational contexts

A fax poll 'Altruism in Corporate America' (Viega and Dechant, 1993) asked the question: 'In the last twenty years, do you think acts of corporate altruism have increased? stayed the same? decreased?' This question was addressed to members of the Academy of Management's Executive Advisory Panel and of the Conference Board Council on Development, Education and Training, who were also asked to obtain responses to this question from a few other executives in their firms. The results were: 52.5 per cent said that altruism had increased, 31.7 per cent said that it had stayed the same, and 15.8 per cent that it had decreased. In terms of the altruism matrix discussed in Chapter 2, the responses revealed that the altruistic practices in the polled organizations were motivated, to a large extent, by 'utilitarian altruism' rather than by 'genuine altruism'.

When we read of the need for altruistic behaviour in the organizational context, we are not surprised because our experience tells us that without generous doses of altruism, life and living in a society would simply be intolerable. We see that altruistic behaviour surrounds our day-to-day personal, family and social lives. As parents, we nurture children and devote ourselves to the needs and cares of the family; as citizens, we are engaged in a host of voluntary community service activities such as Boy Scouts, Girl Guides, and Meals-on-Wheels for older persons and people with disabilities. The early socialization practices in the family, school, and religious contexts inculcate and encourage such behaviours because these are considered to be the moral foundations of personality development. Because altruistic behaviours are considered vital to our moral development, many scholars have proposed a stable dispositional and motivational basis for such behaviour. For instance, Murray (1938) and later Jackson (1967) postulated the need for nurturance as the basis of altruistic behaviour. Likewise, Maslow (1967) suggested that the self-actualizing value of 'goodness', when internalized, may prompt unselfish behaviour. One might then ask: Why is altruism ignored or neglected in the organizational context?

Although altruism as a form of prosocial behaviour stemming from an intrinsic motive has been investigated in both the motivational and social psychological literature (for example, see Mook, 1987; Worchel, Cooper, and Goethals, 1988), such behaviour in organizational contexts has been neglected as a subject of serious scientific study. Instead, management research has centred primarily on the achievement and power phenomena within organizations (McClelland, 1961, 1975; Winter, 1973; Pfeffer, 1981; Mintzberg, 1983) to the complete exclusion of examining altruistic motives and behaviours among organizational members.

There are several reasons which might explain why altruistic behaviour is ignored in business organizations. One reason might be the absence of an altruism construct in the organizational behaviour literature. The other reason might be the societal norms for or expectations of the behaviour of business executives. The third reason might be the cultural and historical forces which have contributed to a form of individualism that is inimical to altruistic behaviour in business organizations. We explore these reasons because through an awareness of them, leaders are better prepared to recognize and assess the obstacles to altruistic behaviours and to develop appropriate strategies to overcome these obstacles.

When we examine the organizational behaviour literature, we find that it has identified and analysed a variety of behaviours in the workplace which contain elements of altruistic behaviour. We refer to activities such as mentoring (Levinson, 1976); Japanese management practices (Pascale and Athos, 1981; Ouchi, 1981); empowerment behaviours (Kanter, 1983; Burke, 1986; Nielsen, 1986; Conger and Kanungo, 1988c); team-building (Dyer, 1977); some forms of organizational spontaneity (George and Brief, 1992); prosocial organizational behaviour (Brief and Motowidlo, 1986); and citizenship behaviour (Organ, 1988). These activities involve actions performed for the benefit of others, but are simply designated and categorized as specific management strategies or practices rather than as a subclass of the larger category of altruism. Thus, the absence of the single unifying construct of altruism has led organizational theorists to overlook the altruistic nature of these activities.

The second reason is the societal norms for or expectations of the behaviour of business leaders. In a study of public attitudes towards altruism or helping behaviour in twenty selected occupations, Rotter and Stein (1971) found executives of large companies were ranked very close to the bottom – that is, perceived as being egotistical. They fared only slightly better than used car salesmen and politicians. And in spite of differences in education and geography, four separate samples of respondents uniformly maintained that executives act in their own self-interest and help others only if they lose nothing by doing so. Such is the stereotype of executives in large corporations. The study also revealed that members of the clergy and physicians were ranked high on altruism, showing concern for the good of others through personal sacrifice. As can be seen, there is a bias in the public mind that executives are self-centred, egotistical individuals. They and their organizations are perceived as economic entities concerned primarily with gaining material advantage for themselves. Their main objective is to make themselves and their organization 'winners' in the cut-throat competition of the free market. To win, executives are expected to protect their self-interest even if it requires harming their competitors.

Thus, managers are viewed primarily as selfish individuals devoid of moral obligations for the interests of others. This selfish nature is seen as the natural outcome of environmental demands. Just as religious and health service organizations promote altruistic behaviour among clergy and physicians respectively, in the service of their clients, industrial organizations are assumed to promote competitive behaviour on the part of executives to benefit themselves and their clients (shareholders, investors, and so on). These expectations have formed the social norms for executive behaviour and have fostered a self-fulfilling prophecy for executives. Perhaps, guided by such norms, executives themselves have been somewhat reluctant to exhibit altruistic behaviour. In the public's attitude, they have found a rational justification for their lack of altruistic concern. The spin-off effects of societal expectations might be that organizational theorists have likewise concentrated on researching executive power and achievement and have largely ignored altruism, in the belief that it is less relevant to the normal functions of an executive.

The perceived irrelevance of altruistic behaviour among executives was most eloquently expressed some time ago by Theodore Levitt (1958) when he observed that 'altruism, self-denial, charity, and similar values are vital in certain walks of life. But for the most part, those virtues are alien to competitive economics' (p. 49). To emphasize his point, Levitt argued that business should never indulge in altruism unless it makes economic sense: 'The governing rule in industry should be that something is good only if it pays. Otherwise it is alien and impermissible. This is the rule of capitalism' (p. 48). In contrast to certain other professions, Levitt (1958) commented that the executive

> whose only aim is personal aggrandizement and whose tactics are a vulgar combination of compulsive demagoguery and opportunistic cynicism is less dangerous than the social evangelist who, to borrow from Nietzsche, thinks of himself as 'God's ventriloquist.' ... There is nothing more corrupting than self-righteousness and nothing more intolerant than an ardent man who is convinced he is on the side of the angels. (p. 46)

The third and, we believe, the more fundamental and possibly the root cause or explanation for the neglect of or indifference to altruism in business organizations is the impact of the sociohistorical forces, which can be analysed from both economic and psychological perspectives. From an economic perspective, organizations are considered most efficient when the classical mechanism of a *laissez-faire* philosophy is at work. The work of Adam Smith ([1776] 1936) and, more recently, Milton Friedman (1963) advocates the notion that a free and competitive market contributes not only to the profitability of the most efficient organization, but also to the good of society. Human selfishness in this context is considered divine providence. The Darwinian notion of 'survival of the fittest' and Jeremy Bentham's hedonistic psychology and utilitarian moral philosophy, emphasizing an 'enlightened self-interest', are often considered ideological justifications for an economic *laissez-faire* philosophy. It is believed that what is true for biological organisms has to be true for economic organisms as well.

Thus the concept of the 'economic' human being has evolved from these intellectual traditions and has become the dogma of the American corporate world. Guided by the desirability of a competitive free market characterizing the external environment and an economic human being characterizing the internal environment, organizations consider it ideal to create conditions that facilitate individual autonomy and complete freedom of choice. In addition, it is acceptable to use information to one's own advantage and to compete intensely among individuals to maximize personal benefits. These conditions simply preclude the possibility of altruistic behaviour.

Although organizations promote selfish and egotistical (rather than unselfish and altruistic) behaviours on the basis of the dual assumptions of free competition and economic human being, both these assumptions have been found to be untrue. Economists such as Galbraith (1967), for instance, suggest that American corporations do not operate in an ideal free market environment. Markets do not control the corporations; rather the corporations control the markets, and consequently are able to engage in monopoly pricing, price cutting to eliminate competition, employment and customer discrimination, deceptive advertising, environmental pollution, and so on. All of these forms of egotistical behaviour at the organizational level directly produce many social 'evils' rather than social 'goods'. They have led to public criticism of business ethics and a public demand for corporate altruism and social responsibility – as can be seen from the findings of a survey by the Canadian Democracy and Corporate Accountability Commission. In this survey, 2000 Canadians were asked whether they agreed with the proposition that: 'Business executives have only one responsibility, to operate competitively and make profits'. Only 20 per cent agreed with this proposition; whereas more than 70 per cent opined that: 'Business executives have a responsibility to take into account the impact their decisions have on employees, local communities and the country, as well as making profits' (Roseman, 2002: 1).

The 'economic' human being assumption has also been challenged by psychologists (McGregor, 1960; Maslow, 1965; Schein, 1980). Contemporary motivation theories suggest that human nature is not limited simply to maximizing personal economic benefits. It is much more complex. It includes both social and self-actualizing tendencies, as Schein's 'complex' human being concept would suggest. Thus, organizational practices that promote individual competition and maximize personal benefits may not be in tune with human nature as we know it today.

In addition to the influence of the economic assumptions of free market and the economic human being, the development of a self-centred psychology in America operates against giving altruism its rightful place in organizational contexts. America has promoted a psychology of the self that Edward Sampson (1988) describes as a 'self-contained' individualism. It is a conception of the self that is based on 'the belief that each of us is an entity separate from every other ... with a sharp boundary that stops at one's skill ...' (Spence, 1985: 1288). It is exclusive of others. Altruistic behaviour, on the other hand, requires a conception of self that is more inclusive of others. As a result, altruism is not perceived as important or as beneficial as it might be in other cultures. Instead, there is a strong emphasis on individual accomplishment and material prosperity, even at the expense of others.

Historically, the evolution of this 'self-contained' individualism can be traced back to medieval Europe (Morris, 1972) and to its crystallization in the sixteenth century (Baumeister, 1987). Before this time, conceptions of the self were of individuals who had only limited control over their environments. External forces played a more determinate role, and the notion of an individual independent of others was quite foreign. For example, in the Greek Oedipus cycle, circumstance rather than personality was central: 'The personal character of Oedipus is really irrelevant to his misfortunes, which were decreed by fate irrespective of his own desires' (Morris, 1972: 4). In contrast, we find an emphasis on individualism and personal control by the time of Shakespeare's tragedies in the Renaissance: 'The fault, dear Brutus, is not in our stars, but in ourselves' (Morris, 1972: 4). These notions of self-authorship and self-contained individualism reached their zenith or most exemplary expressions in the American culture of the twentieth century. Spence (1985) argues that 'individualism is so central to the American character and its positive aspects so taken for granted that it is difficult to conceive of any alternative kind of self-conception' (p. 1287).

The American emphasis on individualism arose largely from the country's early ties to the Protestant work ethic and its emphasis on individual achievement (Weber, 1958). Protestantism brought a relatively radical view of humankind's relationship to God. The glorification of God became the principal aim of one's life and could only be accomplished through productive work. Work was perceived as humankind's calling, and not to work would be to risk falling from grace:

> To lose time, through sociability, 'idle talk', extravagance, even through taking more sleep than is necessary for health (6 to at most 8 hours), is considered worthy of total moral condemnation. Franklin's remark that 'time is money' is not yet found, but the proposition is true, so to speak in a spiritual sense: it is infinitely valuable, since every hour lost is taken away from work in the service of God's glory, hence passive contemplation is also valueless, indeed in some cases actually objectionable.
>
> (Weber, in Runciman, 1978: 141–2)

In this system, the attainment of worldly success through hard work was interpreted as a sign of God's grace. And while strict adherence to this philosophy was perhaps limited in reality, the moral imperatives of working hard, making a success of oneself, and becoming materially prosperous survived (Spence, 1985: 1289). Over time, these beliefs became secularized and incorporated into a national value system. In addition, they combined with a belief that success depended on a measure of individual competition. It was not enough to work hard; the real measure and sign of achievement was to 'win' in the competition against others. Individualism and with it the notion of personal rights and freedom became sacred values. These beliefs and those of the philosophy of the Enlightenment ultimately guided the formulation of the Declaration of Independence and the Constitution. As such, both documents spell out the assumption that the individual is supreme and that government exists to serve the individual and not the other way around: 'We hold these truths to be self evident, that all men are created equal, that they are endowed by their creator with certain inalienable rights' (Spence, 1985: 1287–8). These ideals derive directly from a notion of individualism where freedom is based on personal or individual expression.

These beliefs are so ingrained in our sense of self that children, at an early age, are expected to learn self-reliance and independence (Spence, 1985). For example, parents – especially the fathers of boys – encourage their children to be competitive and to win and to be the best (Block, 1973). Spence (1985) also notes that in our theories of ego and moral development, the highest stage is one in which the individual reaches an autonomous level above the acceptance of and the conformity to standards of society (for example, Kohlberg, 1969; Loevinger, 1976). Such a value system fosters an individualism that is narrowly defined in terms of self-interest. It precludes a sense of self that might be more inclusive, one that would recognize interdependence and a sense of community. At best, it encourages only limited acts of altruism – the utilitarian mode – those which also serve the interests of the actor.

Why is altruism needed in organizations?

As Nobel Laureate Herbert Simon (1990) observed: 'It is of no little moment for the human future whether people are necessarily and consistently selfish, as is sometimes argued in population genetics and economics, or whether there is a significant place for altruism in the scheme of human behavior' (p. 1665). The fact is that there are distinct liabilities to a world view that emphasizes individualism to the exclusion of responsibility to a larger public good. Of course, it cannot be denied that emphasis on individual accomplishment and the notion that 'time is money' have created a fast-paced competitive climate that has brought technological advancement and great material prosperity to Western countries. But it cannot also be equally denied that such progress has not been without a rather heavy price. Examples abound of the unhealthy search for self-interest, as cited in the first chapter.

Furthermore, this sense of individualism might well explain the rise of the 'me generation' – a people trapped in narcissistic self-absorption. In the wake of material prosperity has come a decreased dependence on others, as services, formerly provided by the family or community, are now purchased from the 'care-provider' businesses. Technological advances and geographically dispersed career opportunities have contributed to a more mobile society, which has meant a growing sense of aloneness and alienation. These trends and developments, and their effects, are a powerful, but sad, commentary on the price of egotism which stems from an undue emphasis on the almost unrestrained exercise of individual autonomy and freedom.

What is needed is a greater sense of balance between this individualism and a concern for the larger community. In his book, *The Duality of Human Existence* (1966), David Bakan proposed that each of us has two fundamental but opposed senses: a sense of self that is demonstrated in self-protectiveness and self-assertiveness, and a sense of selflessness that manifests itself in communion with others. Although both are necessary for survival, the difficulty facing individuals and societies is to reconcile these two polar senses. Dawes (1975) characterizes this difficulty as the 'commons dilemma', borrowing the concept from Hardin (1968). In the West, the balance is tilted in favour of self-assertiveness; in the East, in favour of communion. There is a need to move more towards a point of balance, to cultivate a concern for the larger community rather than one of indifference to it. For example, Deutsch's (1973) work on competition and cooperation demonstrated the positive achievements of cooperative groups in which members sought to help an entire group in reaching its goals. Recent research on Japanese and European manufacturing strategies, where collective achievements are rewarded over individual goals, further supports the notion that a more inclusive self can lead to greater effectiveness (for example, Schein, 1980; Ouchi, 1981).

In addition, studies in psychology have shown that striving for individual achievement can often be self-defeating and counterproductive. Spence and Helmreich (1983) found that interpersonally competitive individuals were less likely to achieve than peers who were less competitive. The compulsively driven Type A individual may succeed in the short run only at the expense of their long-term health (Jenkins, Roenman, and Zyzanski, 1974). The phenomenal economic success of Japan and other Asian countries is testimony to the role that a more inclusive self, a more altruistically driven self, can play in increasing rather than decreasing business effectiveness. The rewards of altruism may stretch significantly beyond 'good business sense' to our own personal health and well-being. In a controversial study, Harvard psychologist David McClelland found a surprising link between altruism and the body's immune system. He showed students a film of Mother Teresa working among the poor and sick of India. Afterwards, tests showed increased levels of Immunoglobulin A, an antibody used by the body against respiratory infections. Even students who expressed a dislike for Mother Teresa showed the enhanced immune response (Growald and Luks, 1988). Perhaps the benefits of altruism may be far greater than we realize.

Business organizations in America are in a transition (Salk, 1973), moving from an industrial to a post-industrial stage. The industrial era promoted organizational philosophies of self-centred, competitive relations within the framework of a mechanistic and bureaucratic structure. It also promoted cultural norms and values of personal achievement and independence. The contemporary post-industrial environment, however, is different; it is more complex and turbulent. In order to respond to such an environment, organizations can no longer be viewed merely as economic machines designed for technological progress and for the personal benefit of those who control them. Instead, they must be seen as sociotechnical systems responsive to human needs both in their external and internal environments. As human systems, organizations must develop the moral obligation to respond to the needs of consumers, minority groups, and others in their external environments. In other words, organizational structures and philosophies need to shift towards more organic forms with collaborative relations and a sense of purpose that includes the organization's effectiveness as well as the improvement of the quality of life of its members. The individuals' personal values also need to shift from self-centred achievement and independence to altruistic self-actualization and interdependence.

These value shifts are also evident in debates on technology versus humanism. Scholars argue, much more than ever before, in favour of limiting technological and economic benefits when these are achieved at the expense of human values (Braden, 1970; Reich, 1971). As Mintzberg (1982b) points out, 'economic morality' cannot be promoted if it amounts to 'social immorality'. Such trends in the thinking of management scholars clearly attest to the need for promoting altruism in organizations.

The sources of spiritual strength

The preceding discussion reviewed the formidable obstacles to the very ideas of moral altruism, and much more so to its practice in the business organization. It also pointed out that the need for altruism and altruistic behaviours is equally great – a need for the attitude of solidarity. For the charismatic leader, the attitude of solidarity is, unquestionably, an ethical imperative. As discussed in Chapter 2, solidarity is the attitude '... in which the common good properly conditions and initiates participation, and participation in turn properly serves the common good, fosters it, and furthers its realization' (Wojtyla, 1979: 284–5). How then can charismatic leaders prepare themselves and their organizations to meet the challenging demands of their role? As discussed in Chapter 4, charismatic leadership is essentially transformational in nature – that is, the self-transformation of the leader and of the followers. The strength and resources needed for this purpose go well beyond the mere material domain; leaders need to draw upon their inner spiritual strength, upon their spirituality. The sections that follow explore the nature of spirituality and its manifestation in the cognitive, affective, and moral character of the individual; the nature of charismatic leadership in the context of the spiritual experiences of both the leader and followers when its practice is consistent with moral principles. The chapter concludes with some observations on the sources which the spiritual sages of all time recommend that leaders can draw upon for the spiritual strength, solace, and inspiration they need in order to exercise leadership that is uplifting both to themselves and to their followers.

Spirituality – its nature and manifestations

The Concise Oxford English Dictionary defines 'spiritual' as '... of spirit as opp. to matter; of the soul esp. as acted on by God; ... inner nature of man' (1964: 1236). It defines 'spirit' as the 'Intelligent or immaterial part of man, soul' (1964: 1236). These meanings suggest the dual natures, material and spiritual, of human beings. However, it was clearly recognized, as far back as Aristotle, that the union between spirit (soul) and matter is so perfect that only one being is present. Just as a piece of pottery is not clay plus the shape in which it is formed, but shaped clay, in the same manner, philosophical tradition that goes back to Aristotle and Aquinas has always regarded a human being not as a body plus a spirit (soul), but as matter made real by a spirit (soul), resulting in a unique person.

The human being as a whole person functions through the use of the intellect and the will. The intellect uses the external sensory inputs (sight, hearing, touch, taste, smell) and internal mental processes (memory and imagination) to penetrate into those deep levels of reality that the physical senses and processes cannot access; it does so through abstract concepts and ideas that help to make sense of and give meaning to things, events, and people that one observes and experiences, and with which one interacts. The will is the power that acts in the light of intellectual knowledge. Although the cognitive and volitional behaviours occur in the spiritual domain they are, nevertheless, influenced – that is, facilitated or hampered – by the material nature of human beings. For example, rhetoric can be used to arouse the imagination that can either elucidate or detract from rational arguments. Likewise, the hedonistic inclinations of our material being influence our emotions, which can, in turn, make it easy or difficult for us to act as our intellect directs. The faculties of intellect and will that are unique to human beings enable us to ascend from the domain of sense experience to the domain of thought – to a higher reality which Plato termed as the 'eternal' unchanging objects of thought – ideas (Adler, 1981).

Assuming the existence of an ideational domain in human life, how do we describe the concept of spirituality and its place in that domain? If we search for its meaning in the various religions of the world, spirituality is a concept which is difficult to define in a manner that is universally acceptable. Since the contents of religious beliefs and rites differ widely from age to age and from one society to another, it might be difficult to arrive at a consensus on what constitutes spirituality. However, if we analyse the spiritual experience *per se* and its behavioural manifestations among individuals of different religious persuasion instead of looking into specific religious beliefs and rites, it becomes self-evident that there is much accord on the understanding and appreciation of the essence of spirit at three levels: cognitive, affective, and manifest behaviour levels. The commonality of the spiritual experience at each of the three levels transcends the diversity of religious practices and beliefs. Like material objects, spirituality is also experienced, comprehended, felt and acted upon. It is the experience of reality at a deeper level, or at a higher level of abstraction. It is experiencing the incorporeal, or the symbolic reality underlying the mundane phenomena.

The cognitive and affective levels of spiritual experience

At a cognitive level, spiritual experience represents a realization that, at the core of human existence, there is a set of cardinal virtues and capital vices, and that the goal of human life is to live these values and overcome the vices.

The idea of virtue as signifying human rightness was taken for granted by the contemporaries of Socrates. Plato first formulated the four cardinal virtues – *prudence, justice, fortitude*, and *temperance*.

> This particular intellectual framework, the formula which is called the 'doctrine of virtue', was one of the great discoveries in the history of man's self-understanding, and ... has become a basic component of the European consciousness, as the result of centuries of persistent intellectual endeavor by all the creative elements of the emerging West, both the Greeks (Plato, Aristotle) and the Romans (Cicero, Seneca), both Judaism (Philo) and Christianity (Clement of Alexandria, St. Augustine).
>
> (Pieper, 1966: xi)

These virtues are termed *cardinal*, the Latin word for 'hinge', because around them hinge human acts or practices which acquire moral significance when they are consistent with the moral principles implicit in the cardinal virtues. The cardinal virtues conform to the order or dictates of reason and, unlike the technical jargon usual in the sciences, these virtues are expressed in words that are frequently used in ordinary conversation, thereby confirming that these ideas 'constitute the vocabulary of everyone's thought' (Adler, 1981: 3).

At an affective level, the spiritual experience represents complete trust and dependence on such virtues that represent a set of human values or an agent who embodies these values. In its most sublime manifestation, spiritual experience represents a complete identification with the values (or the agent) with a view to achieve an enduring blissful state of existence. The Hindu religious tradition, as expressed in the *Vedas*, describes this state as '*sat-chit-anand*' – that is, true and blissful consciousness. The Christian religious tradition refers to it as a mystical union – the most sublime experience of the Divine in this life. Phenomenologically, spiritual experience represents a cognitive and affective sense of inner being, an inner experiential ego state or a kind of consciousness that is different from the day-to-day experiences of the self in relation to its material nature or to the material world.

Thus, there is nothing mythical or unreal about spiritual experiences. On the contrary, such experiences are real. They are psychologically mediated in the sense that individuals experience spirituality when they identify with or are committed to a set of values or to an agent symbolizing these values. In Maslow's theory of meta-motivation (1967), the spiritual experiences of pursuing values such as truth, goodness and beauty are regarded as a major part of one's self-actualization. In terms of the need-theoretic approach, spiritual experience results from the satisfaction of cognitive needs by discovering truth, altruistic needs by doing good to others, and aesthetic needs by appreciating beauty in nature or in human works of art. In Hinduism, spiritual experience implies the realization of Satyam – that is, truth; Sivam – that is, goodness; and Sundaram – that is, beauty (Radhakrishnan, 1962).

When we think of truth, goodness, and beauty, we are thinking about the world in which we live, '... about the knowledge we have of it, the desires it arouses in us, and the admiration it elicits from us' (Adler, 1981: 24). In addition to need satisfaction, the values underlying truth, goodness, and beauty are so transcendent and universal that these ideas also become the touchstone by which we judge our manifest behaviours, discussed in the next section.

Spiritual experience at the level of manifest behaviour

How is the spiritual experience expressed in one's manifest behaviour? What are the sources of the norms, principles and standards of human behaviour in the spiritual domain? Responses to these questions generally come from the prescriptions of moral science or ethics. In Chapter 2, we discussed the nature and conditions of a morally good act. We now explore how a morally good act is necessarily an expression of a spiritual act and an indispensable condition of a truly spiritual experience.

The ability to distinguish between morally good and evil acts is critical to the formation of character which enables the individual to behave consistently in moral ways, and reveals to the observer the individual's visible moral identity. As Bass and Steidlmeier (2004) observed:

> An approach to ethics based upon moral character and virtue enjoys an extraordinarily broad cross-cultural base ... that guide ethical discourse in cultural settings as diverse as Western and Confucian traditions. From Plato's 'philosopher king' to the virtuous Confucian minister of the state, the 'moral sage' and the 'superior person' are portrayed as both a font of wisdom and the embodiment of virtue, whose very presence and being bring about personal and social transformations. (p. 186)

However, the knowledge of ethical principles alone (as criteria for distinguishing between good and evil acts) is futile unless the individual makes the effort to habitually incorporate these principles in his/her behaviour. As Walton (1988) observed: 'Character is more than what simply happens to people. It is what they do to themselves' (p. 175). It constitutes an inner-directed and habitual strength of mind and will. The acquisition of such habitual strength, also known as 'the practice of virtue', is greatly facilitated by the individual's moral mentors, who guide both by precept and example. 'Both Socrates and Confucius ... proposed to his followers the highest ethical standards that they themselves implemented in their own lives. More important, in terms of authenticity, each was recognized as a sage and leader by others, not by self-proclamation' (Bass and Steidlmeier, 2004: 186). Since practice makes perfect, it is imperative, in character formation, that much thought and care is given to what one practices. Because the values underlying the cardinal virtues, referred to earlier, are universally accepted, we shall briefly discuss each cardinal virtue in the context of its importance to moral behaviour.

Prudence: The practice of this virtue requires the habitual assessment, in the light of right standards, the situation or issue on which a decision is to be made. The assessment also includes the likely favourable and unfavourable consequences of the decision for oneself as well as for others. The leader who is in the habit of practising prudence will not abdicate his or her responsibility for unethical behaviour by followers through messages such as: *do whatever you have to do, just don't tell me about it.* The prudent person will not only not resent that others disagree with his or her views, but will actively seek such information to better assess the situation and exercise sound judgement. In other words, prudence means the objective assessment of the situation and the exercise of sound judgement.

Justice: The virtue of justice requires the individual to strive constantly to give others what is their due. The 'due' is interpreted to mean more than the legalistic concept of the contractual rights of others. It includes whatever others might need in order to fulfil their duties and exercise their rights as persons – that is, the right to life, to cultural and moral goods, material goods, and so on. In the organizational context, it means the exercise of a sense of responsibility that balances, in a fair manner, the rights of all the stakeholders – customers, employees, suppliers, government, community, as well as of the owners.

Fortitude: It is the courage to take great risks for an ideal which is worthwhile. A courageous person faces difficult situations and strives to act positively to overcome obstacles in order to do what is good and noble. One of the underlying characteristics of fortitude is perseverance and endurance against great odds. As Leavitt (1986) observed: 'Determined people try to make it happen because they believe in it, not because the odds are on their side' (p. 95).

Temperance: The practice of this virtue involves distinguishing between what is reasonable and necessary, and what is self-indulgent. Although it includes the reasonable use and satisfaction of one's sense appetites, it also involves the efficient and effective allocation of one's time, effort, and resources. In essence, temperance means the exercise of self-control which, in general, would lead one to avoid and resist the temptation to over-indulge in hedonistic behaviours. 'Temperance or intemperance of outward behavior and expression can have its strengthening or weakening repercussion on the inner order of man' (Pieper, 1966: 204).

The practice of virtues reflects the individual's struggle with two fundamental, but diametrically opposed, choices that constantly confront the individual in every context of his/her life. These choices are: (a) should my thoughts and actions be for my benefit at the cost of others? or (b) should my thoughts and actions be for the benefit of others at my cost? The values inherent in the choice of 'other before self' are universal and form part of the heritage of all cultures. This point was illustrated in Chapter 2 with examples from two religious cultures, the west European and Hindu, which have fundamentally different approaches to the sources of religious truth that illuminate the path to moral behaviour. In the context of the charismatic leadership phenomenon, the transformational role adopted by the charismatic leader requires a principal concern for the benefit of others, even when such concern involves considerable cost to the leader. This is so because the leader's personal sacrifices become the authentic, visible signs of commitment and dedication to his/her ideal vision, which is one of the critical factors that moves the followers to attribute charisma to the leader.

To recapitulate the discussion so far. Spiritual experience is not an aberration. It is of the very essence of human beings to function in the spiritual domain. In order to so function, the individual's behaviour tends to be governed by the habitual practice of virtues. In the final analysis, it is the spiritual experience that enables each person to grow and fully realize the tremendous potential that is unique to that person. 'Of all living creatures, only humans have the power to shape their own character, to choose between honourable and dishonourable behavior, to tell the truth or deceive, to exploit or respect others, to work hard or slack off. Each decision so shapes the person that subsequent behavior is more predictable' (Walton, 1988: 176). If a good moral character is of the essence of every human being, then with much greater reason does it become so of charismatic leaders who, by their 'vision, values, and determination add soul to the organization' (Leavitt, 1986: 222–3).

Charismatic leadership – its spiritual dimensions

As discussed previously, the charismatic leadership phenomenon is characterized by the following features. First, it is a relational phenomenon whose existence depends primarily on the followers' experience of dependence on the leader as an influencing agent. Second, in this relationship, followers develop a strong emotional bond with the leader characterized by an abiding faith and an unwavering trust. Third, very often, the development of such an emotional bond with the leader is triggered by the followers' experience of some contextual crises that have affected them personally. Finally, charismatic leadership comes into being when the followers perceive and attribute certain characteristics to the leader such as the embodiment of idealized vision, extraordinary abilities, and unconventional behavioural manifestations.

These characteristics of the charismatic leadership phenomenon are also echoed in our spiritual experiences. In almost all religions, spirituality is associated with a belief in relating oneself with a higher-order influencing agent. The relationship is one of dependence on this super-human/supernatural agent manifested in different forms in different religions. For some, the agent is perceived to be another human, a guru – the supreme teacher, or a saint, who embodies to a high degree of perfection all the good and noble qualities that human beings can aspire to. Some even perceive the physical manifestations of nature itself to be so overpowering that they develop a dependence on it with awe and wonder. For others, the agent is conceived as an abstraction in the form of God, the Supreme Being, omniscient, omnipotent and omnipresent; in some religions, such an agent is an impersonal being, in others a personal being.

In this dependent spiritual relationship, followers of various religions also experience a strong emotional bond with the agent and demonstrate unconditional trust and unquestioning faith in the agent to guide their behaviour. Regardless of the form in which the agent is perceived, the followers attribute extraordinary idealized, and visionary qualities to the agent. Furthermore, while relating to an idealized agent, it is not uncommon that the spiritual experiences of dependence, trust, faith and so on among the followers of various religions might also be triggered by the experiences of crisis in their life.

Although there is this surface resemblance, in the religious contexts, between our experiences of charismatic leadership and spirituality, such resemblance does not necessarily imply that the leadership phenomenon has a spiritual dimension to it. In order to demonstrate the spiritual dimensions of the charismatic leadership phenomenon, one has to consider the psychological nature of our experiences of both the leadership and the spirituality phenomena and uncover the relationship at a much deeper level. For this purpose, we need to consider the different components of the leadership phenomenon each of which contains a spiritual dimension. These components are: the spirituality in leadership experience; the rituals that reinforce the leader's influence; the self-identity of the leader; the leader's exercise of power and the use of empowering practices. Our focus here is on the spirituality in leadership experience, the leader's exercise of power, and the use of empowering practices.

Spirituality in leadership experience

In the history of mankind, religious leaders and social reformers have continually experimented with new forms of values and ideals to improve the existing conditions. In the organizational context, the leadership role has been viewed as the role of managing meanings since organizations are systems of shared meanings (Pfeffer 1981; Smith and Peterson, 1988). Charismatic leaders provide meaning to organization's goals, ideologies and values and strive to achieve them by establishing a new order that replaces the old one. One central religious belief in Hinduism, as stated in the *Bhagavad Gita*, asserts that when from time to time, the world gets engulfed in vice through the acts of evil agents, God takes human form to eliminate vice and vindicate virtue and the virtuous, thereby establishing peace and order for mankind. Such beliefs reinforce the idea that in the eyes of the followers, the charismatic leaders who are committed to achieve their professed idealized vision are like a God-figure. The followers tend to identify with their leaders and internalize the ideals and values professed by the leaders. The psychological outcomes of the self-growth oriented identification and internalization processes represent the spiritual experiences of the follower – at both the cognitive and emotional levels.

For the leaders, on the other hand, the formulation of an idealized set of values that constitutes the vision – that is, the meaning they create for the organization, and their commitment to the realization of this vision, represent the spiritual experience. Most religious leaders develop their vision of the perfect, the idealized and eternal dharma or righteousness after being exposed to the limitations, imperfections, sorrows and suffering, of the finite environment – as in the case of a Buddha, or a Francis of Assisi. Reflections on the experiences of the imperfect material world give rise to the spiritual experience of the perfect idealized representation of the world.

Charismatic leaders in a non-religious context go through a similar process: from experiencing the limitations of the status quo to the experiencing of an idealized state or a vision for the future that is discrepant from the status quo. The cognitive realization of an idealized vision is a profoundly transforming spiritual experience. The essence of the experience is that transformational or charismatic leaders identify with or personally relate to a set of values that raise them to 'higher levels of motivation and morality' (Burns, 1978: 20). The leaders' commitment to higher levels of morality and their self-actualizing motivation to achieve the vision is often manifested in the leader's fortitude or in the form of taking personal risks and making personal sacrifices. Although personal risks and sacrifices by themselves do not necessarily indicate spiritual experience, what is noteworthy is that the transforming spiritual experience resulting from the leader's commitment to the idealized vision becomes a powerful motivational force to bear and, even gladly, suffer the hardships and sacrifices that may be necessary.

Spirituality and power

The charismatic leaders are known to engage in socialized rather than personalized power. Socialized power is expressed in self-controlled and altruistic ways for the service of others, whereas personalized power is expressed in impulsive, aggressive and self-aggrandized ways for one's own benefit (McClelland, 1985). The exercise of socialized power by the leader thus implies that the leader practises the cardinal virtues and takes personal risks and makes personal sacrifices for the benefit of the followers. The need to exercise socialized power forms a significant part of the spiritual self of the moral person. On the other hand, the effort to gain material wealth and status through personalized power and the hedonistic attachment to such outcomes is the product of *eros* (in Western traditions) or *kama* (in Hindu traditions) in the competitive self-centred, individualized self, and not of the spiritual self.

The path to the realization of the spiritual self, as prescribed in the eight beatitudes of the Sermon on the Mount (Mathew 6 and 7) or in other religious scriptures, essentially involves that the individual act simultaneously on two fronts. The individual regards the mundane world as transitory or illusory, *maya* in the Hindu tradition, and, therefore, develops an emotional detachment from it. At the same time, the individual develops a bonding with the spiritual reality which alone has permanence, is unchanging and endures. Emotional detachment allows the leader to develop prudence and the proper perspective of the purpose and role of people, things, and events. The bonding with the spiritual reality that results from the leader's commitment to the higher purpose, and the emotional detachment from the mundane reality enables the leader to overcome personal vices and to cope with sorrows and sufferings.

Furthermore, the leader views these events as a rich source of inner strength and insights of the human condition which are essential if the leader is to adopt the needed compassion for and understanding of his/her followers. As Roland (1988) puts it, 'As the person becomes increasing involved in the realization of the spiritual self, he or she still relates to others and fulfils responsibilities, but without the intense looking to the other for the fulfilment of wishes, esteem and the desire to be needed' (p. 307). In other words, the need for socialized power and the manifest behaviours to fulfil such needs on the part of the charismatic leaders through personal sacrifices are the reflections of their increased involvement in the spiritual self and their detachment from the individualized self.

Spirituality and empowerment

As discussed at length in Chapter 4, the nature of the influence of charismatic leaders on the followers is characterized as transformational rather than transactional. The followers achieve self-transformation not through transactions in social exchange of valued resources, but through the emotional bonding, identification with the leader and internalization of the idealized vision advocated by the leader. The primary objective of bringing about the self-transformation in the followers is to enable them to achieve an inner strength or a set of cognitive beliefs regarding their capability to pursue and be involved in the realization of the vision.

In influencing the followers to achieve the inner strength and capability, the actions of charismatic leaders are designed to 'empower' the followers. The experience of being empowered by an influencing agent, who is strong and virtuous, trustworthy, supportive and nurturing, is a spiritual experience. The followers' dependence on such an agent does not imply a mindless, servile, or parasitic subordination. It rather implies a dependence which is of the nature of a growth-oriented identification with the leader that allows followers to draw inspiration from the leader in order that they might be self-efficacious and, like the leader, achieve a similar self-transformation. Charismatic leaders do not force followers to be dependent on them. Therefore, the followers' dependence does not result from fear of rejection or other forms of threats. Instead, charismatic leaders lead by personal examples of virtuous acts and by the idealized content of the vision the attraction of which is greatly enhanced by the inspirational manner in which it is articulated. The followers are, thus, inspired to follow the leader's example and they do so with complete autonomy and of their own volition. They choose to be dependent on the leader because they are convinced that the path they follow will eventually lead to the realization of their own deepest hopes and aspirations.

The nature of this dependence is similar to that of a serious student who trustingly follows the guidance and direction of the teacher in order to grow and develop into an independent exponent of the subject matter. Such dependence is best exemplified by the *chela-guru* (student-teacher) relationship in Hindu asceticism. In this relationship, the guru is revered and almost worshipped as a godhead. Through this reverence and worship the students seeks the guru's blessings in order that they might attain to the level of knowledge, wisdom, and spiritual development of the guru. In fact, a prayer commonly used by students to obtain such blessings is: 'Oh Lord, through your grace the mute speaks and the lame conquers the mountain. I pray thee for your grace'. The prayer obviously has a spiritual connotation; the student seeks to be empowered. The empowering experience that underlies this relationship has a strong spiritual element that substantially affects and forms the student's spiritual life. In much the same way, the follower depends on a charismatic leader for self-transformation.

In conclusion, although leadership can take various forms, such as: task, people oriented, participative, and charismatic or transformational leadership, it is only when leadership takes the charismatic form, that the spiritual dimension comes much more to the fore. In the task, people and participative leadership roles, the leader neither pursues any idealized vision, nor attempts any growth-oriented self-transformation. The self-identity of such leaders can be characterized in terms of an emphasis on either individualized 'I-ness' self (task-oriented leadership role) or familial we-self (people and participative oriented leadership roles). But one can notice the presence of the spiritual self when true leadership is exercised – that is, when the leader brings about change in the status quo through the growth-oriented self-transformation of the leader and of the followers.

At the cognitive level, the spiritual dimension of the self is expressed in the sense of the profound consciousness of the eternal values of truth, beauty and goodness represented by the vision of the leader. At the affective level, spirituality is manifested in the emotional bonding with and trust and faith in these values. At the manifest behaviour level, spirituality radiates primarily through the leader's virtuous life that places the interest and concerns of others before those of one's self, despite the personal risks and sacrifices that may be and, in fact, are inevitably involved.

The development of the leader as a moral person

The development of the leader for ethical leadership revolves principally around character development. Through the habitual practice of the cardinal virtues, leaders acquire the inner-directed and habitual strength of mind and will to incorporate moral principles in their behaviour, and thereby form their character. As discussed previously, charismatic leadership is essentially transformational in nature – that is, the self-transformation of the leader and of the followers. The leader is a role model to the followers in respect of both task performance and ethical behaviour. Undeniably, the leader is indeed the soul of the organization, whose beliefs, values and behaviours influence and shape, for better or worse, the organization's moral environment, and has all encompassing serious ramifications both within and outside the organization. For this important reason, the focus of the discussion will first be on the self-transformation of the leader.

The basic competencies in managerial resourcefulness

The nature of the tasks that leaders perform does not significantly differ in kind with those involved in managerial jobs. However, leadership involves tasks that can be described as non-specific, complex, discretionary, relatively unstructured, and subject to constant change. What are the specific skills that leaders need? After a review of the research in the past two decades on the nature of managerial jobs and skills, Kanungo and Misra (1992) found that the studies agree on the nature of managerial jobs, but lacked a coherent scheme to understand and identify the core skills components. They proposed an alternative conceptual framework that focuses on managerial re-sourcefulness, which include both skills and competencies.

According to this framework, skills are overt behaviours that are task-specific, suitable for routine or programmed tasks and for a stable environment. Competencies refer to intelligent functioning and the abilities to engage in cognitive activities that are person-generic dispositions that are necessary for non-routine or unprogrammed tasks and for a complex volatile environment. The competencies that mediate the utilization of the task-specific skill are: affective competence, intellectual competence, and action-oriented competence. As components of resourcefulness, the competencies are the learned abilities of managers to employ self-regulating and self-controlling procedures on their jobs. Thus, affective competence is the self-regulation of emotions and feelings; intellectual competence is the self-regulation of thought processes and beliefs; and action-oriented competence is the self-regulation of intentions and actions.

An empirical study involving 485 managers found a positive correlation between resourcefulness and managerial success as measured by income level. Factor analysis of items reflecting resourcefulness revealed four factors: *proactive analytical orientation, problem-focused perseverance, emotional equanimity*, and *goal-directed orientation* (Kanungo and Menon, 2005). The items forming the first three factors reflect the competencies suggested by Kanungo and Misra (1992). Thus, proactive analytical orientation items reflect intellectual competence, problem-focused perseverance items reflect action-oriented competence, and emotional equanimity items reflect affective competence. The fourth factor, goal-directed orientation, reflects the tendency to have a goal at all times. Now, individuals who possess the affective, intellectual, and action-oriented competencies are clearly those who are goal-oriented at all times. The goal-directed orientation is implicit in each of the three competencies and can, therefore, be regarded as an overarching dimension of these components of managerial resourcefulness. A valid and reliable scale for measuring these competencies has been developed by Kanungo and Menon (2005) – refer to Appendix II.

To return to the question posed at the beginning of this section – what are the specific skills that leaders need? The discussion on managerial resources strongly suggests that leaders need to have three competencies, in addition to specific task-related skills. These competencies are: affective competence, intellectual competence, and action-oriented competence. Expressed in terms of the findings of the empirical study, we can say that effective leaders are those who have an overall *goal-directed orientation*, along with *proactive analytical orientation, problem-focused perseverance*, and *emotional equanimity*. These competencies or orientations are essential for effective leadership because the tasks that leaders face are often non-specific, complex, discretionary, relatively unstructured, and subject to constant change.

Morality and managerial resourcefulness

The earlier discussion on cardinal virtues concluded that the practice of virtue enables leaders to incorporate moral principles in their behaviour, and thereby form their character. The competencies or orientations, just discussed, bear a striking correspondence to the four cardinal virtues. We now explore the nature and significance of this correspondence in the context of leadership in organizations.

Goal-directed orientation is the tendency of the individual to have a goal at all times. This orientation corresponds to the virtue of justice. Organizations entrust leaders with responsibility for a variety of issues, and resources – human, materials, financial. Justice requires that leaders utilize these resources efficiently and effectively with due regard to the rights of all the stakeholders involved. This responsibility can be properly exercised only when the organization's goals and objectives consistently guide the leaders' decisions in respect of these issues and resources. The practice of the virtue of justice facilitates the development of a goal-directed orientation.

Proactive analytical orientation involves the intellectual competence to assess the situation and plan a course of action through analytic and synthetic thinking that serves the organization's goals and objectives. The leader's exercise of this competence is greatly enhanced by the practice of the virtue of prudence. Prudence requires that the individual habitually assess, in the light of right standards, the situation or issue on which a decision is to be made. For this purpose, the prudent leader will keep an open mind, actively seek relevant information, and conduct a dispassionate analysis in order to exercise sound judgement.

Problem-focused perseverance involves the action-oriented competence to perform the tasks and activities, including attention to details and time frame, needed to achieve the goal despite the overwhelming difficulties and obstacles one may encounter. The practice of the virtue of fortitude gives leaders the courage to take risks, to face difficulties and work at overcoming obstacles in the pursuit of a worthwhile goal.

Emotional equanimity relates to the affective competence that involves self-regulation of emotions and feelings. As one undertakes the various tasks involved in goal attainment, it is normal to experience failure as well as success. The affective competence enables individuals to learn and grow from both their failures and successes. The practice of the virtue of temperance enables leaders to exercise restraint and discipline in order that irrational expression of emotions do not cloud their judgement and prevent them from viewing persons, things and events in their proper perspective.

Are virtues and managerial resourcefulness mutually exclusive?
The cardinal virtues enable leaders to habitually incorporate moral principles in their behaviour. The practice of these virtues involves the exercise of the basic competencies critical to managerial resourcefulness and, as a consequence, strengthens the basic competencies. However, the continued exercise of the basic competencies does not guarantee that these will be done in a virtuous manner. There are criminals who have exceptionally high goal-directed orientation, proactive analytical orientation, and problem-focused perseverance. It is only when these competencies are exercised consistent with moral principles that the practice of virtue is reinforced. The cardinal virtues are the 'hinges' on which the basic competencies acquire moral significance. The competencies of managerial resourcefulness are the necessary but not sufficient condition for the practice of virtue. Leaders provide ethical leadership when they exercise the basic competencies in the pursuit of virtue.

The leader's need for personal mastery

The leader's exercise of the basic competencies in managerial resourcefulness, consistent with moral principles, contributes to the moral development of the leader. However, ethical leadership requires that leaders also prepare themselves to foster and promote an ethical environment in the organization; and this involves contributing to the transformation of the followers. The following description of a leader by Lao-Tzu aptly and succinctly makes the point that the leader's life is best epitomized by the dictum: 'others before self' – at all times and regardless of the cost to self.

> A leader is best when people barely know he exists. Not so good when people obey and acclaim him. Worse when they despise him. If you fail to honour people, they fail to honour you. But of a good leader, who talks little, when his work is done, his aim fulfilled, they will say 'We did this ourselves!'
>
> (Lao-Tzu, quoted in Bynner, 1962: 34–5)

For this purpose, it would be helpful to consider the notion of 'personal mastery' which is one of the critical disciplines of the 'learning organization'. According to Peter Senge (1990), a learning organization is one where '... people continually expand their capacity to create the results they truly desire, where new and expansive patterns of thinking are nurtured, where collective aspiration is set free, and where people are continually learning how to learn together' (p. 3). Creating a learning organization would indeed be the objective of ethical leaders. To achieve this objective, the leader first acquires personal mastery and then assists and empowers all employees to do the same. We briefly explore the critical elements of personal mastery –

shared vision, objective assessment, focused energies, creative tension (Senge, 1990).

Shared vision: Leaders with high personal mastery devote much effort and care to ensure a shared vision for the organization – one that incorporates the beliefs, values, and aspirations of the employees, who are seen and treated as valued members of the organization's community. The employee-organization relationship is that of a covenant and 'rests on a shared commitment to ideas, to issues, to values, to goals, and to management processes' (de Pree, 1989). In such a relationship, there is no tradeoff between economic success and moral principles. Rather, adherence to moral principles constitutes the organization's higher purpose. Such a broad vision promotes among employees a better understanding and appreciation of and feel empathy for each other that moves them away from self-centredness. 'Individuals committed to a vision beyond their self-interest find they have energy not available when pursuing narrower goals' (Senge, 1990, p. 171).

Objective assessment: Leaders with high personal mastery cultivate a culture of openness that permits a meaningful dialogue and sharing of information, and the testing of assumptions pertaining to acceptable behaviour and practices in the organization. At the same time, it enables employees to assess their work situations objectively, recognize the interdependencies that exist, and thereby, better understand and appreciate the structures, practices and relationships in the organization, as well as the business and economic realities in which the organization operates. Underlying the objective assessment is a deep commitment to a continuous search for truth in the sense of desire to recognize reality as it currently exists.

Focused energies: Leaders with high personal mastery see an intrinsic value in the vision – as an expression of the organization's purpose, as the *raison d'être* for the organization's existence. They pursue the vision with focused energies and total dedication of their talent, ability and efforts. Even when their efforts to realize the vision suffer serious setbacks and failures they do not abandon the principles implicit in the vision. They see setbacks and failures as opportunities for learning, and their deep faith in the vision, in its intrinsic value causes them to persevere with steadfast determination; and, *despite* the personal costs that might be involved, they continue to strive towards the vision.

Creative tension: The vision is a desired future state. It is inherent in the very nature of the vision that it is discrepant from the current reality as revealed by objective assessment. The discrepancy between the vision and current reality can lead to discouragement, anxiety, fear of failure, and even hopelessness. This uncomfortable, if not painful, experience can generate in leaders considerable pressure to compromise the integrity of the vision, to lower the established standards that reduce the demand on the leader's efforts and performance. The prospect of relief from the emotional upheaval by lowering the vision becomes an attractive option. However, leaders with high personal mastery will not succumb to seeking relief from the emotional tensions by following the line of least resistance and avoiding the pressures to struggle towards the vision. Instead, they view the 'vision-current reality gap' as creative tension and manage it through self-control and self-regulation. They seek and work towards the good that is inherent in the vision not because it is comfortable or convenient, but because it is the honourable and right thing to do.

The elements of personal mastery closely correspond to the cardinal virtues and the basic competencies of managerial resourcefulness. Indeed, the practice of these virtues and competencies are indispensable to acquiring personal mastery. For this reason, leaders with high personal mastery are more likely to exhibit a disciplined pattern of behaviour that is guided by a deep personal vision and enduring moral principles. As alluded to, at the beginning of this section, the learning organization comes about when employees at all levels acquire personal mastery. What can leaders do to encourage and assist their followers to acquire personal mastery? As Peter Senge observes: '... be a model. Commit yourself to your own personal mastery. Talking about personal mastery may open people's minds somewhat, but actions always speak louder than words. There's nothing more powerful you can do to encourage others in their quest for personal mastery than to be serious in your own quest' (1990: 173). The next section explores the sources of self-transformation necessary for personal mastery.

The principles of ethical power for the self-transformation of leaders and of followers

The inspiring and practical principles of ethical power – *purpose*, *patience*, *persistence*, *perspective*, and *pride* – proposed by Blanchard and Peale (1988) are important sources of self-transformation of leaders and of followers. These principles, aided by the habitual practice of *examination of conscience*, enable leaders to behave ethically, to consistently do what is right despite the insurmountable pressures so often inherent in a difficult situation. Leaders can tap these sources of ethical power to acquire personal mastery to develop as a moral person possessed of inner strength and resourcefulness that leads to the self-transformation of both the leader and of the followers.

The principles are consistent with and integral to the cardinal virtues and the basic competencies of managerial resourcefulness. As discussed in this section and summarized in the following table, adherence to these principles requires the practice of the virtues and the basic competencies reinforced by the practice of regular examination of conscience. The table also depicts two outcomes of the practice of these principles – the leader's personal mastery, and pride – that is, the high self-esteem that originates from the followers' efforts and accomplishments.

Table 5.1   The sources of self-transformation of leaders and followers

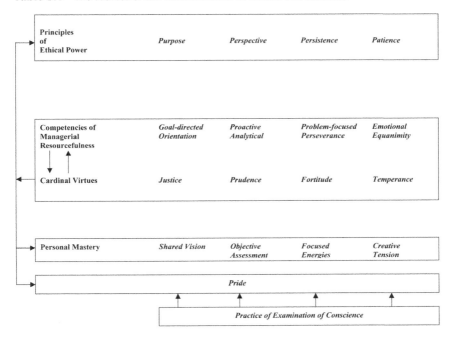

Source: Mendonca (2001)

Purpose

The critical set of leader behaviours are to evaluate the status quo, to formulate and articulate a vision that is discrepant from the status quo, and to take the means, which are: personal sacrifice, building trust among followers, and using unconventional behaviour, to achieve the vision (Conger and Kanungo, 1998). Leaders draw on their ethical power when they see the vision as a 'calling', a reflection of one's genuine aspirations rather than a leadership technique, when they subject the vision as well as the means to achieve it to the rigorous scrutiny of the higher purpose that the vision serves. In the context of the business organization, it is universally admitted that it must be profitable. But, ethical leaders ponder whether profits are a means or an end in itself. Corporations committed to a higher purpose '... exist to provide society with the goods and services it needs, to provide employment, and to create a surplus of wealth (profit) with which to improve the general standard of living and quality of life' (O'Toole, 1985).

The powerful influence of the higher purpose in providing a proper perspective on profits and related issues can be seen from the debate and its outcome at Merck and Co. over mectizan, a breakthrough medicine for the treatment of river blindness that is endemic in 35 countries across 3 continents. The company was faced with three issues. First, the people who desperately needed this medicine were the least able to pay for it. Second, if the company donated it, then it might create an expectation of future donations and discourage research in this area. Third, the added cost from the potential risk in the event of adverse side effects from the drug.

While these issues were being debated by the company and the world public health community the ravages of river blindness continued. The debate ended when the company recalled the following words from the address of George W. Merck, the company's president, to the Medical College of Virginia, in 1950: 'Medicine is for the people. It is not for the profits. The profits follow, and if we have remembered that, they have never failed to appear ... How can we bring the best of medicine to each and every person? We cannot rest until the way has been found with our help to bring our finest achievements to everyone.' These core values moved the company to decide that it would donate mectizan for the treatment of river blindness to all who need it for as long as needed (Merck and Co., 2000: 12).

The scrutiny of the vision in the perspective of its higher purpose will cause the leader to practice primarily the virtues of prudence and justice, aided by the managerial competencies of goal-directed and proactive analytical orientations. The practice of prudence will cause leaders to habitually assess situations and problems in the light of moral standards, of consequences of their decisions for organizational members and society at large, rather than the leaders' self-serving goals. The practice of justice requires that leaders recognize their duties and responsibilities, and to strive constantly to balance in a fair manner the rights of all the organization's stakeholders. The practice of prudence and justice in the pursuit of the leader's vision will not only strengthen the leader's moral character, but would also enhance the followers' perceptions of the leader's trustworthiness. They will see their leader effectively model the elements of personal mastery – in particular, commitment to shared vision and objective assessment.

Patience

As leaders work towards the realization of the vision, they are certain to face obstacles from the environment – internal or external, or from the reluctance of the followers to accept and be committed to the vision. It takes time and effort to overcome such obstacles that are inevitable in a worthy and noble endeavour. Hence, the need for patience. Leaders bear the present difficulties with calm and serenity because of their faith in the vision. They develop an inner realization that 'in good time' the difficulties will be resolved. This realization or faith is not the fatalism that inevitably paralyses action. Rather, it is the leaders' conviction that the vision is worthwhile that contributes to their constancy of purpose and leads them to continue undaunted with what needs to be done. To maintain one's faith in the vision and stay the course, leaders need to habitually exercise prudence, fortitude and temperance, and develop the competencies of proactive analytical orientation, problem-focused perseverance, and emotional equanimity.

The practice of prudence enables the leader to properly assess all facts and circumstances surrounding one's decisions, and the practice of fortitude develops the capacity to act positively in the midst of difficulties. The relevance of prudence for leadership is reflected in the leader's need to be sensitive to the environment; the relevance of fortitude is demonstrated by the fact that the leader is called upon to perform behaviours that involve great personal risks and sacrifices (Conger and Kanungo, 1998). The relevance of temperance arises from the fact that this is precisely the time when leaders need self-control that is critical to one's inner calm and serenity. The practice of prudence and fortitude is the source of patience that gives leaders the strength to refrain from unethical actions and behaviours when things do not go as planned – even though 'everyone is doing it'. These virtues and competencies enhance the leaders' capacity for objective assessment of reality and to work diligently to realize the vision that are critical elements of personal mastery.

Persistence
The power of persistence is best captured in Winston Churchill's bulldog-like perseverance – 'Never! Never! Never! Give up!' However, persistence does not mean a stubborn obstinacy. It means that leaders do not allow difficulties to weaken their resolve to 'stay the course'. Instead, they continue to take the steps necessary, even those involving personal risk and sacrifice, to achieve the vision. The practice of fortitude strengthens one to strive to overcome difficulties not because it is convenient or pleasant to do so, but because one's duty requires that it be done. This idea is forcefully expressed by John Hoyt Stookey of National Distillers, now Quantum Chemical, when he declared: 'One of the things ... that we mean by ethical behavior is that we will forego profit in order to adhere to a standard of conduct. I believe that's a message a CEO needs to convey loud and clear to an organization and I find myself doing that' (quoted in Watson, 1991: 186). The practice of fortitude is facilitated when leaders develop the competency of problem-focused perseverance that, in turn, permits them to model effectively their quest for personal mastery.

Perspective
To see events in their proper perspective means an objective assessment of their importance in the light of the vision. The habit of reflection is critical to

acquiring a sense of perspective. And reflection is simply not possible unless one devotes some time each day to silence – a resource that has been recommended by the wise of all time and from all cultures, and yet the one resource that remains most untapped. Silence is more than refraining from noise; it is the inner silence that allows one to reflect on the higher purpose, to question one's decisions in the light of that purpose, and to seek strength not to betray it. It allows one to listen to the inner stirrings of the spirit, and is needed to make distinctions between right and wrong, to discern what one ought to do. The quest for personal mastery requires some form of 'meditation' or contemplative prayer because '. . . it is helpful in working more productively with the subconscious mind' (Senge, 1990: 164).

Pride

The leader obviously needs to have high self-esteem that originates from a legitimate pride in one's accomplishments. Ethical leaders exhibit pride but do not indulge in vanity. The dividing line between pride and vanity is unbelievably thin because of our strong egotistic tendencies, but ethical leaders recognize that inordinate self-love is a human vice and not a virtue. Ethical leaders do not view achievements as the result of their own endeavours deserving of self-adulation; rather, as 'our achievements' – the fruits of the leader-followers effort and collaboration. Such a view, is a natural outcome of the leader's 'other-centredness', and generates two effects. First, the emphasis on 'our achievements' has a powerful positive influence that is highly energizing to the followers. Second, such a visible expression of the leader's 'other-centredness' reinforces in the eyes of the followers the leader's belief and commitment to moral altruism.

The ethical leader's self-esteem also originates from the esteem of one's followers. However, the leader's behaviours are not designed to merely gain the acceptance of the followers. For example, in formulating the vision the leader considers the needs and aspirations of the followers, but does not allow the desire to be accepted by the followers to compromise the vision, when such compromise will jeopardize the organization's higher purpose. In other words, the leader does not look to the followers for affiliative assurance (Boyatzis, 1984) to reinforce his or her self-love, but strives to assist followers to internalize the vision and work to realize it. Apart from the pressure from the followers, leaders will always experience a gap between the current reality and the vision. Undoubtedly, the gap creates much emotional tension that could be eliminated by lowering or compromising the vision. Leaders with high personal mastery recognize that this gap is a powerful source of energy for creative change (Senge, 1990). The habitual practice of prudence and temperance aided by the competencies of proactive analytical orientation and emotional equanimity will enable leaders to acquire and model personal mastery in seeing current reality objectively and in managing the emotional tension created by the vision-reality gap.

The practice of examination of conscience

The preceding discussion has touched on several suggestions available to leaders in their efforts to develop the inner strength they need to function as ethical, moral persons. However, the enduring effectiveness of these suggestions depends upon their habitual practice and, more importantly, on setting aside a specific time for the practice of examining one's conscience. It is a fact of human experience that we do not suddenly find ourselves engaging in grave and serious unethical practices. Rather, such grave practices are preceded by minor unethical lapses that we might rationalize as acceptable because these are so inconsequential or that 'everyone is doing it'. As Plato observed; 'The life which is unexamined is not worth living' (in Bartlett, 1968: 92). The examination of conscience – the scrutiny of behaviour in the light of the higher purpose, prevents unethical behaviour, or at least alerts us to the fact that we might be treading on its slippery slope.

The development of a moral environment

When asked about his primary job, the chairman of Matushita Electric said: 'To model love. I am the *soul* of this company. It is through me that our organization's values pass' (Blanchard and Peale, 1988: 89). Indeed, the leader creates the organization's moral environment, but it cannot be created by the fiat of the leader. The statements of the vision, mission, and policies, however numerous, well crafted, and articulated, are futile if the leader's actions and behaviour are inconsistent with these statements. Indeed, actions speak louder than words; what the leader does and values set the ethical tone and create the moral environment of the organization. In the 1988 Touche Ross survey of key business leaders, deans of business schools, and members of Congress about ethical standards and behaviour, '... 73 percent recognize the CEO's ability to influence ethical behavior' (Kangas, 1988: 11).

'Personal virtue and moral wisdom of the leader provide the checks and balances upon power and self-aggrandizement ... The heart of the moral enterprise is the development of good character, which is defined by commitment to virtue in all circumstances' (Bass and Steidlmeier, 2004: 188). The organization's moral environment is a natural overflow of ethical leadership manifested by the leader's altruistic motive, empowering influence strategies, and moral character formation. The practice of personal mastery through the exercise of virtue and managerial resourcefulness ensure ethical leadership through the leader's commitment to ethical principles and values that is expressed not only in terms of intellectual assent, but also in the leader's continuous struggle to live by them. As Aristotle said: 'We are what we repeatedly do. Excellence then is not an act, but a habit.' Truly, the leader is the *soul* of the organization. For example even in the relatively trivial area of employees' work attendance, the CEO's example has been found to be critical. In one organization, when the CEO regularly attended his office at 10.00 am, his executives came in at 9.45am, but when his successor began work at 7.00am these same executives now came in at 8.00am or earlier (Stovall, 1988). However, there are other more telling examples: One manufacturer continued to produce a product known to cause illness and death; on the other hand, Johnson & Johnson immediately withdrew Tylenol from the market, at enormous costs, even though the product was completely safe (Lank, 1988). The actions of these CEO's sent clear, unambiguous messages about the ethical standards expected from their employees.

The higher purpose established for the organization by the charismatic leader becomes the starting point in creating the moral environment. The higher purpose and the values it represents convey to the followers what is acceptable and unacceptable behaviour. However, to facilitate the employees' internalization of these values, the leader must develop specific codes of conduct for organizational members. The codes of conduct are useful and even necessary, but care needs to be taken in their development. For instance, in a survey of codes of conduct of more than two hundred companies, the '... most ignored item was personal character – it seemed not to matter' (Walton, 1988: 170). In addition to the codes of conduct, the leader should identify areas and issues that might be particularly susceptible to unethical conduct, and develop internal policies and processes that specifically deal with them.

The leader should also create opportunities for employees to exchange ideas and experiences in the implementation of the code of conduct, as well as the difficulties they might likely encounter in acting ethically in certain situations – especially if ethical dilemmas are involved. Some organizations hold periodical 'retreats' or discussion forums which provide employees with the intellectual, emotional, and moral support necessary to maintain the high ethical standards expected of them.

Codes of conduct, related policies and procedures, and support structures are undoubtedly essential to the development of the organization's moral environment. However, in the final analysis, it is the charismatic leader's personal conduct that determines the effectiveness of the codes, policies and procedures, and the support structures. The moral environment cannot be created by the *fiat* of the leader. Just as Mother Teresa's work for the 'poorest of the poor' is an external outpouring of her love for God, in much the same way, the organization's moral environment is a natural overflow of the charismatic leader's commitment to ethical principles and values that is expressed not only in terms of intellectual assent but also in his/her daily struggle to live by them. Indeed, a moral leader '... engenders virtue in self, others, and society through example and virtuous conduct' (Bass and Steidlmeier, 2004: 188).

Ohmann (1989) cites the example of an executive whose policies and practices flowed naturally from his beliefs and values. This executive believed that his talent and resources are gifts entrusted to his stewardship for the '... maximum self-development and useful service to one's fellows in the hope that one may live a rich life and be a credit to his Creator ... it is against this frame of reference that the decisions of the moment easily fall into proper perspective' (Ohmann, 1989: 66–7). As a result, he provided employees with opportunities to develop to the fullest their potential. He held his employees accountable but, at the same time, coached them to performance levels that would justify the higher rewards. He viewed profits as a measure of the successful use of the potential of his employees. Instead of talking about employee communication programs, he spent most of his time in the field listening to his employees. He managed conflicts not by considerations of expediency or self-concern but by reference to what best served the organization's higher purpose. His basic values not only led to consistency in his decisions and behavior that made him dependable and trustworthy, but also gave meaning and significance to even the otherwise routine and inconsequential activities of the workplace. The resulting moral environment truly reflected the *soul* of the organization and enabled its members to internalize its values which became a firm and enduring foundation for their ethical behaviour.

Conclusion

The discussion in this chapter examined the nature of spirituality and its manifestation in the cognitive, affective, and moral behaviour or character of the individual. It is of the very essence of human beings to function in the spiritual domain, and the commonality of the spiritual experience transcends the diversity of religious practices and beliefs. At the cognitive level, spiritual experience represents a realization that, at the core of human existence, there is a set of cardinal virtues and capital vices, and the goal of human beings is to live the virtues and overcome the vices. At the affective level, the spiritual experience represents a state of blissful existence resulting from complete trust and dependence on these values or on an agent who embodies them. At the level of manifest behaviour, the spiritual experience is expressed in the individual's moral behaviour resulting from a struggle with two fundamental, but diametrically opposed, choices – action for the benefit of self at the cost of others versus action for the benefit of others at the cost of self.

In order to uncover the relationship between the phenomena of spirituality and charismatic leadership, we explored the different components of the leadership phenomenon which contain a spiritual dimension. We saw that the spiritual self is present in the leadership role of bringing about change in the status quo in order to achieve an idealized vision through the self-transformation of the leader and of the followers. At the cognitive level, spirituality is expressed in the sense of the profound consciousness of the eternal values incorporated in the leader's vision. At the affective level, it is manifested in the emotional bonding with and trust and faith in these values. At the manifest behaviour level, it radiates through the leader's virtuous life that places the interest of others before those of one's self, despite the costs that may be involved. In the light of this discussion, it is clear that spirituality is the quintessence of charismatic leadership. It explains its underlying strength and provides the leader with the means to develop as a moral person and to create the organization's moral environment that is conducive for ethical behaviour. As Confucius observed: 'He who exercises government by means of his virtue may be compared to the north polar star, which keeps its place and all the stars turn towards it' (Analects, 2:1, in Bartlett, 1968: 71).

Suggested questions for reflection

- What are the reasons for the obstacles to altruism in the organizational context?
- What is the nature of spirituality? How is it manifested in the cognitive, affective, and moral behaviuor of the leader?
- How can the exercise of charismatic leadership become a source of spiritual experiences?
- What are the practices that enable the leader:

    → to develop as a moral person?
    → to create the organization's moral environment that is conducive for ethical behaviour?

6 Cultural contingencies of leadership

Synopsis

In this chapter, we discuss the culture-fit of the leader role behaviours and the leadership influence process in the context of non-Western societal cultures. We first propose a conceptual framework that identifies the major cultural dimensions that might facilitate or hinder leadership effectiveness; and also discuss a leadership mode that is more appropriate to overcome the cultural constraints. We then explore the question of whether the cultural norms and values that prevail in non-Western societies are compatible with the moral values that are inherent in the altruistic ethic. This discussion demonstrates that, although the major religions that have shaped the cultural norms and values of non-Western societies might have different and even contradictory theological insights and responses to this question, there is a remarkable consensus on the ethics of human behaviour; it would seem that the norms of moral behaviour are deeply ingrained in human nature.

Introduction

The leadership phenomenon has played a dominant role, for better or for worse, in the functioning of groups, organizations, and institutions in every human society. Previous chapters have discussed the modal orientations in leadership, the ethical dimensions in leadership motivation and leadership influence processes, and some approaches to preparing for ethical leadership. This discussion, however, has been in the sociocultural context of Europe and North America. The study of leadership along cross-cultural dimensions has received little attention. For instance, we do not know what sociocultural characteristics facilitate or hinder leader effectiveness, in what way do societal cultures influence the nature of the leadership function and the leader's role behaviours (Dorfman, 1994). With the increasing globalization, the knowledge of the influence of culture on leadership effectiveness has now assumed greater importance for the management of organizations in general, and multinational corporations in particular. It is equally, if not more, important for public and private sector organizations in developing countries because the introduction of change and its sound management depends, to a considerable extent, on the efforts and initiatives of leaders in these organizations.

Hence the need of this chapter. More specifically, we explore the cross-cultural studies of the trends or modalities of leadership with a focus on the emerging modal orientation in leadership. Since the previous chapters considered leadership primarily in terms of the Western ethos, the discussion in this chapter will be developed in the context of the Eastern and South Asian cultures, norms and values, in particular, those of the developing countries. We examine the culture-fit of the leader role behaviours and influence processes relative to these cultures. We also examine the compatibility of the prevailing cultural norms and values with the altruistic ethic which, we have argued, is critical to effective leadership.

Influence of culture on leadership effectiveness

The discussion on leadership research in Chapter 3 identified four major leader roles, task, social, participative, and charismatic; and two leadership influence processes, transactional and transformational. Each leadership role serves the organization and its members in an unique manner. The task, social, and participative roles are directed at the effective supervision and maintenance of the status quo; whereas the charismatic role serves to bring about the transformation of both the members and the systems of the organization. In the task, social and participative roles, the leader ultilizes mostly the transactional influence process; whereas in the charismatic role, the leader utilizes the transformational influence process. However, when we discuss how cultural variables influence leadership effectiveness, we shall consider both the leader role and the social influence process that is characteristic of the role. For this purpose, we first propose a conceptual framework that identifies the major cultural dimensions which might facilitate or hinder leadership effectiveness in developing countries.

The earliest research efforts on organizational leadership across cultures involved simple questionnaires measuring a range of attitudes and actions of managers without creating theoretical frameworks to demonstrate how research results might be explained across cultures (Haire, Ghiselli and Porter, 1966; Bass and Burger, 1979). Following these initial studies, several scholars have developed conceptual schemes to study organizational behaviour in cross-cultural contexts (Kanungo and Jaeger, 1990; Hofstede, 1993; Trompenaars, 1993; Triandis, 1994). The most influential among these have been the work of Hofstede (1980), who identified four cultural dimensions:

individualism/collectivism, power distance, uncertainty avoidance, and masculinity/femininity.

> *Individualism* 'implies a loosely knit social framework in which people are supposed to take care of themselves and their immediate families only, whereas *collectivism* is characterized by a tight social framework in which people distinguish between in-groups and out-groups; they expect their in-groups (relatives, clan, organizations) to look after them, and in exchange for that they feel they owe absolute loyalty to it'. (p. 45)

> *Power distance* is 'the extent to which a society accepts the fact that power in institutions and organizations is distributed unequally'. (p. 45)

> *Uncertainty avoidance* is 'the extent to which a society feels threatened by uncertain and ambiguous situations by providing career stability, establishing more formal rules, not tolerating deviant ideas and behaviors, and believing in absolute truths and attainment of expertise'. (p. 46)

> *Masculinity* denotes 'the extent to which the dominant values in society are "masculine", that is, assertiveness, the acquisition of money and things, and not caring for others, the quality of life, or people'. (p. 46)

These dimensions have proved useful for the study of organizational behaviour across cultures. Other scholars (Earley, 1993; Traindis, 1993; Erez, 1994) have probed in depth the individualism/collectivism dimension which has considerably improved its power to explain cross-cultural behaviour.

Using several cultural dimensions, Kanungo and Jaeger (1990) developed a conceptual framework which derives managerial assumptions about work attitudes and behaviour from the sociocultural characteristics. Such a model, Figure 6.1, provides a reasonably comprehensive framework to explain the internal work culture of organizations in developing countries.

It will be seen from this figure that compared to the developed countries, the sociocultural environment of developing countries is characterized by: relatively high uncertainty avoidance and power distance; and relatively low on individualism and masculinity. These dimensions are as suggested by Hofstede (1980). On the additional dimension of 'abstractive versus associative thinking' suggested by Kedia and Bhagat (1988), developing countries are relatively low on abstractive thinking and high on associative thinking.

The sociocultural environment determines management beliefs, values,

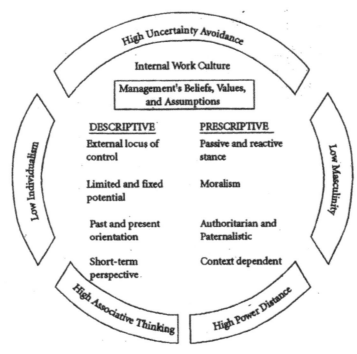

Figure 6.1 Characteristics of the internal work culture of organizations in non-Western societies in the context of their sociocultural environment
Source: Kanungo and Jaeger (1990)

and assumptions of workers and work behaviour that characterize the organization's internal work culture. As seen in the figure, the internal work culture of developing country organizations can be broadly categorized as: (a) the descriptive assumptions about human nature; and (b) the prescriptive assumptions about the guiding principles of human conduct. The descriptive assumptions relate to: causality and control of outcomes; creative potential and malleability; time perspective; and time units for action. The developed and developing countries differ significantly on each of these dimensions. Thus, relative to the developed countries, managers in developing countries are more likely to assume that their employees: have an external locus of control; have relatively fixed potential and are not easily malleable; operate from a time perspective that is past and present-oriented; have a short-term focus (Kanungo and Jaeger, 1990).

The prescriptive or normative assumptions relate to: adopting a proactive or reactive stance to task performance; moral or pragmatic basis to judge success; people orientation – collegial/participative or authoritarian/paternalistic; operating from predetermined principles or according to the exigencies of the situation. In this category too, there are substantial differences between the developed and developing countries. Thus, in the developing countries, managers are more likely to: encourage a passive or reactive stance to task performance; judge success on moralism derived from tradition and religion; favour an authoritarian or paternalistic orientation; accept considerations of the context override principles and rules (Kanungo and Jaeger, 1990).

The model in Figure 6.1 provides a coherent approach to integrate the sociocultural characteristics of developing countries and the internal work culture of organizations in these countries. Its elements serve as anchors on which to ground one's exploration and understanding of the influence of cultural variables which might suggest that one leadership role is more appropriate and effective than another, and the reasons why this might be so. However, it is recognized that the implications of this model has not been fully explored in the existing literature. Although these culture dimensions and conceptual frameworks seem relevant for the study of the influence of culture on leadership roles in the context of developing countries, the specific ways in which these could be used have yet to be determined. However, initial attempts in this direction have been made. The sections that follow examine these attempts with respect to the four leadership roles previously identified.

Influence of culture on task and social leader roles

Although, the task and social roles have been explored in terms of cross-cultural research (Sinha 1980, 1990; Bond and Hwang, 1986), perhaps, the most in-depth research along these lines has been conducted by Misumi (1985) over the last 40 years in Japan. Initially triggered by contacts with Kurt Lewin, Misumi developed an extension of the Ohio State leadership model peculiar to Japanese culture (Misumi and Peterson, 1985). He discovered that effective supervisors in Japan are those who scored high in team maintenance (consideration) and in team performance (task). The scales he used in Japan correlate very highly with the Ohio State measures (Peterson, Maiya, and Herreid, 1987; Peterson, Smith and Tayeb, 1987). The findings of these studies are consistent with the sociocultural context of Japan. Nevertheless, in interpreting these findings, the sociocultural characteristics of Japan were not explicitly used to explain the findings. For this reason, Misumi's findings would seem to transform what has been a contingency theory in American settings into a normative one for Japan.

In contrast to Misumi's work, Sinha (1990) explicitly used cultural variables to study the effectiveness of task and social leader roles in Indian organizations. Starting with the proposition that India has a collectivistic culture (Hofstede, 1980), the basic premise of his study is that organizational

members expect: personalized relationships, direction and support, and superior-subordinate rather than a peer relationship. From these premise, he
argues that a 'nurturant-task' leadership would be more effective in manager-
subordinates interaction in Indian organizations. The rationale for his argument is that the nurturant-task leader '. . . cares for his subordinates, shows
affection, takes personal interest in their well being, and above all is committed to their growth' (Sinha, 1980: 55), but provides this nurturance only
after subordinates perform the agreed job tasks.

The nurturant-task leader begins by providing clear, specific directions
and performance standards supported by guidance and directions which
subordinates expect. As subordinates accomplish the job tasks, they experience two critical sets of outcomes: (a) nurturant support from the manager;
and (b) enhanced self-confidence in meeting job goals and increased job
competence. With continued success in meeting job goals, the subordinates
gradually seek less direction and feel more capable of assuming responsibility.
At this stage, the nurturant task leader provides less direction and more autonomy, but continues with the nurturant approach and expectations of task
performance at the agreed levels. The repeated cycle of task performance and
increased autonomy exercised by subordinates is reciprocated by nurturance
and reduced direction by the leader. This process results in '. . . a relationship
of understanding, warmth, and interdependence, leading to higher productivity and better growth of both the subordinates and the leader' (Sinha,
1990: 253).

As we can see from Figure 6.2, which depicts the nurturant-task leadership process in a developing country context, nurturant-task leadership has
the potential to move the manager-subordinate relationship from a state of
total subordinate dependence on the manager – as in t1, through a stage of
greater autonomy for the subordinate – that is, a gradual participative approach (NT/P) – as in t2, to a fuller participative approach (P) as in t3. The
nurturant-task leadership process envisages the possibility that eventually – as
in t1, subordinates can be developed to operate as relatively autonomous
groups. The model also recognizes the possibility of the manager-subordinate
relationship regressing into an authoritarian mode – as in t2. This might
occur for two reasons. One reason is that managers attribute the successful job
accomplishments, in t1, entirely to their direction and guidance and, therefore, are apprehensive that reducing such direction would jeopardize
productivity.

The other reason is that the subordinates' desire for more autonomy in t2
might be perceived by the managers as a threat to their authority and position
which is regarded as relatively more significant in cultures characterized by
high power distance. The Kanungo and Jaeger (1990) model also suggests that
developing countries tend to be more collectivistic and high on power distance which further reinforces the point that the effectiveness of task and

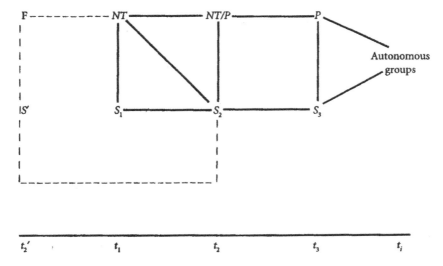

Figure 6.2   Nurturant-task leadership process in a developing country context
Source: Sinha (1990). Reprinted by permission
NOTE: S = subordinate; F = authoritarian; NT = nurturant-task; NT/P = combination of nurturant-task and participative; t = time point. Solid lines indicate positive nature/direction of relationship, and broken lines indicate negative nature/direction of relationship.

social leadership in developing countries will be considerably enhanced by adopting Sinha's nurturant-task leadership model. Dorfman (1994), for much the same reason, has speculated whether the nurturant-task leadership model might not also be appropriate for organizations in countries such as Mexico, Iran, and Korea whose cultures are also collectivistic, high on power distance, and value hierarchical and personalized relationships.

Influence of culture on participative leader role

The rationale underlying participative leadership stemmed primarily from the sociologists' approach to reduce employee alienation or a sense of power-lessness which employees were believed to experience when conditions in the workplace neither allow workers to exercise freedom and control, nor provide them with the opportunity to utilize their potential (Blauner, 1964; Shepherd, 1971). Psychologists (Kanungo, 1982; Sashkin, 1984) have also found em-ployees to become alienated if a work situation constantly frustrates an in-dividual's need for autonomy and control. The problem with participative leadership develops when it is used as a technique to 'share power' on the assumption that all employees seek and want power and its corresponding responsibilities (Thibaut and Kelly, 1959; Emerson, 1962; Blau, 1964; Ho-mans, 1974). Clearly such an assumption ignores the individual's motivational state. Since all employees do not have the identical salient needs, the indiscriminate adoption of the participative technique does not enhance the leader's effectiveness. On the other hand, the participative leader behaviour is effective when the workers' belief in self-determination (Deci, 1975) or personal self-efficacy (Bandura, 1986) is high.

The explicit use of cultural variables to study their influence on the participative leadership role has been explored in two empirical studies. One is a study of US and European managers (Jago, Reber, Bohnisch, Maczynski, Zavrel, and Dudorkin, 1993). It found that participation scores were higher for low power distance cultures than for high power distance cultures. The other is a study of US and Turkish supervisors (Kenis, 1977). The findings of this study was also similar: supervisors in low power and low uncertainty avoidance cultures are more likely to engage in participative decision-making than those in high power and high uncertainty avoidance cultures. Using the Kanungo and Jaeger (1990) model, Figure 1, discussed earlier, Mendonca and Kanungo (1994) explained the impact of the sociocultural environment of developing countries and of the internal work culture on the adoption of participative management in organizations in these countries. According to the model, the sociocultural dimensions of high uncertainty, low individualism, high power distance, low masculinity and high context-sensitive thinking are likely to inhibit participative leadership because the attitudes and behaviours that result from these characteristics are incompatible with participative decision-making. This incompatibility is further aggravated by the organization's internal work culture which results from management's descriptive assumptions about human nature, and their normative or prescriptive assumptions about the guiding principles of human conduct. In the paragraphs that follow, we first consider the influence of sociocultural variables, and then the influence of the internal work culture on participative leadership effectiveness in developing country organizations.

Impact of sociocultural variables

The characteristic of high uncertainty avoidance induces subordinates to be reluctant to exercise autonomy and accept responsibility which, in turn, leads the manager to exercise greater control and provide more detailed directions than are actually required. In low individualism cultures, family concerns and group achievements take precedence over the individual's work concerns and achievements. Since the accomplishment of job objectives is not the primary preoccupation of employees, much less will they desire to be involved in the decision-making related to their job tasks. The high power distance characteristic reflects the societal norm that inequality, expressed in status differentials, is part of the human condition. In the organizational context, it implies that managers and subordinates accept and operate from their respective positions in the hierarchy, and the subordinate's obedience and compliance is not based on a rationale of expertise or competence, but simply on the authority inherent in the manager's hierarchical position. Such status differentials do not promote participative decision-making.

The low masculinity characteristic, with its strong emphasis on sensitivity to people and relationships, implies that the satisfaction of affiliative needs, which are more salient than the need to achieve, takes precedence over satisfaction derived from meeting job objectives. Consequently, low masculinity inhibits the effective implementation of participative management which presupposes that employees seek to fulfil their growth needs on the job through the exercise of control and responsibility on the job, completion of meaningful tasks, and task relevant interactions. The high associative or context-sensitive thinking will also inhibit the effectiveness of the participative leadership role because this cultural characteristic implies that individuals' behaviour is determined not by the logic of principles, but by the needs of the context that is salient to them. The salient context might be attending to one's personal and social obligations during work hours even at the cost of neglecting one's job tasks and responsibilities.

Impact of internal work culture

When managers assume that their subordinates' locus of control is external, then they will logically conclude that their subordinates do not have much confidence in their ability to control events and outcomes, and that they will be reluctant to exercise autonomy, to accept responsibility for problem solving, and generally to be involved in decision-making. In the context of such assumed reluctance, managers will believe it to be futile to practice participative leadership. The same reluctance to practice participative leadership results from managers' assumption that their subordinates have limited potential and that they are not easily amenable to change and development. Believing that their subordinates do not have high job-related growth needs, managers will not put in the developmental effort to prepare subordinates for participative decision-making. The past and present-orientation rather than a future orientation, and a short-term rather than a long-term perspective, influenced by the highly unpredictable and uncontrollable economic and political events (Triandis, 1984), also inhibits participative leadership. With such a time orientation and perspective, one is not inclined to invest effort, time and resources whose returns cannot be realized in the short term. Participative management, and the resulting participative leadership role, essentially requires a future orientation.

The passive or reactive stance to job tasks, largely the effects of low masculinity and low individualism characteristics of the sociocultural environment, is also not compatible with participative management which calls for a proactive or assertive task orientation, to assume control and responsibility for goal setting, decision-making, problem solving, and initiating appropriate measures to bring about the needed organizational change. The authoritarian and paternalistic norm which reflects the high power distance that prevails in the sociocultural environment is not conducive to participative leadership for the same reasons as high power distance, discussed earlier in this section. The last normative assumption which characterizes the internal work culture of developing countries is to allow the exigencies of the situation to determine one's behaviour. This norm that behaviour be context-dependent reflects the associative thinking characteristic of the prevailing sociocultural environment, and carries with it the identical adverse impact on participative management.

Clearly, participative management cannot be *imposed* in an organization irrespective of the sociocultural environment in which the organization operates. The success of participative management depends upon the employees' motivational state which, in turn, is largely the result of the employees' belief in self determination (Deci, 1975) or their personal self-efficacy belief (Bandura, 1986). When employees do not feel capable to cope with the demands of participative management, they will not be motivated to engage in it. The preceding discussion has demonstrated that, other things being equal, the sociocultural environment of developing countries is not conducive to participative management. In addition, the success of participative management depends upon the managers' willingness to engage their subordinates in this mode – that is, allow them to exercise autonomy and responsibility in relation to their job tasks. The managers' descriptive and prescriptive assumptions about human nature and work be-haviour, which generally characterize the internal work culture of developing country organizations, would suggest that they are unlikely to engage in the participative management mode.

In these circumstances, participative leadership becomes a viable option for developing countries only to the extent and degree to which its implementation modalities address the cultural constraints and build on the cultural facilitators. The nurturant-task leadership model and related process proposed by Sinha (1990) demonstrates how managers can exercise the participative role by building upon the cultural facilitators. For instance, the model (see Figure 6.2) postulates that subordinates can be developed to a state of preparedness for participative management – even to the point of functioning as autonomous work groups. However, the model does not propose strategies to overcome the constraints of high power distance and the authoritarian and paternalistic norms which, it recognizes, might prevent managers from fully adopting the participative mode. The cultural contingencies of the charismatic leadership role, discussed in the next section, provides a much more comprehensive treatment of strategies to both build on the cultural facilitators as well as overcome the cultural constraints.

Influence of culture on the charismatic leader role

The charismatic leadership role has not yet been studied systematically in the cross-cultural context. However, the emergence of a model of charismatic leader role behaviour (Conger and Kanungo, 1998), has made possible the cross-cultural analysis of this leadership role. Furthermore, as the following discussion argues, the behavioural contents of this role are absolutely critical for organizational leaders in developing countries. The reason is twofold. First, the behaviours exhibited in this role are today considered as exemplary expressions of missionary or change-oriented rather than the supervisory or status quo-oriented leadership. Second, this role is associated with societal and organizational change of a more radical nature. The magnitude of problems which developing countries face today dictates that it is precisely these parts of the world that can ill-afford the luxury of maintaining the status quo; they do indeed have the greatest need for transformation and radical change. The charismatic leadership role has the greatest potential for significant change and development and, therefore, is the role that is eminently suitable for organizational leaders in developing countries.

In discussing the influence of culture on the charismatic leadership role, we shall use the three-stage charismatic leadership process model of Conger and Kanungo (1998), which has been described in Chapter 3.

Charismatic or transformational leadership

The issue of culture fit

Besides the complex and unpredictable economic, legal and political environments of developing countries, a number of sociocultural dimensions will operate as contingency variables for leader effectiveness. As suggested by Kanungo and Jaeger (1990), developing countries tend to be high on power-distance (hierarchical social structure and authoritarian socialization practices), high on collectivistic orientation (extended kinship networks), and high on religious traditionalism (a moral and reactive rather than a pragmatic and proactive orientation). This constellation of sociocultural features influences the nature of leadership and supervisory behaviour, and the leader-follower relationship. For this reason, the mode of implementing the charismatic leadership must build on the cultural facilitators and overcome the cultural constraints – more specifically discussed in the sections that follow.

The authoritarian socialization practices in developing countries make the relationship between leaders and their followers more personalized rather than contractual. The nature of this personalized relationship can take two distinct forms: (a) affective reciprocity; or (b) manipulative ingratiation. A relationship characterized by affective reciprocity manifests itself in the leader's affectionate and nurturance behaviour toward followers and in the followers' deference and loyalty to the leader. Furthermore, an affective reciprocity relationship often builds an inner strength and self efficacy among followers because of the supportive coaching influence of the leader. This type of relationship is conducive to achieving both personal and organizational objectives. A relationship characterized by manipulative ingratiation, on the other hand, is manifested through a superficial affection for followers on the leader's part, but underlying it, is a basic distrust of the followers. In return, followers similarly exhibit a superficial loyalty but experience more deeply a sense of rejection of and animosity towards the leader. As a result, manipulative ingratiation develops in followers a fragile self-esteem and ego-defensive tendencies. This type of relationship only fosters the desire to achieve personal goals at the cost of organizational goals.

Sinha (1980) suggested that the affective-reciprocity type of relationship is observed among supervisors who exhibit nurturance-task leadership styles. However, as noted earlier, the nurturant-task leadership process envisages the possibility of the leader regressing to the authoritarian mode. This is so because, as the process gets under way, the leader might feel or sense a loss of control over the followers' actions because of a lack of confidence and trust in them. On the other hand, as it will soon become clear, in the charismatic leadership process, the initiative for the development of the affective-reciprocity relationship originates and rests with the leader. The charismatic leadership process identifies the conditions under which the affective-reciprocity relationship is successful and the strategies the leader needs to adopt in order to promote and strengthen this relationship. Thus, an essential condition is the development of the personal self-efficacy beliefs of the subordinates. For this purpose, the leader must first demonstrate confidence in the followers' ability to handle various tasks (Eden, 1990), and then utilize empowering strategies such as coaching, modelling, stating performance goals as worthy ideals, and encouraging and rewarding excellence in performance (Conger and Kanungo, 1998).

The charismatic leader would not engage in strategies which characterize the manipulative-ingratiation relationship – for example, the use of 'lording' strategies. In these strategies the nature of the leadership influence process is chiefly transactional – thus, the leader: literally 'extracts' follower compliance in exchange for rewards and sanctions; places an excessive emphasis on follower's performance failures to foster follower dependence; and conceals or restricts the flow of information to retain control over followers. The ultimate effect of lording strategies is to create the followers' dependence upon the leader and to ensure their personal loyalty without any regard and, often, at the total neglect of the organization's objectives. On the other hand, the leadership influence process which underlies empowering strategies is transformational. As in all leadership, the followers do come to depend upon the charismatic leader, but such dependence is for the purpose of increasing their task competence and their personal growth and development. Moreover, the loyalty to the leader is motivated by the followers' commitment to the organization's vision and its objectives, which they have internalized and for which they accept ownership.

The second contingency variable for leadership effectiveness is the collectivistic orientation among organizational members in developing countries which creates a family ethos of embeddedness in kinship or social networks. This results in a strong 'we-group' and 'they-group' identity, and the associated feelings of trust of the 'we-group members' and distrust for the 'they-group members'. In managerial and leadership practices, such attitudes can inevitably translate into nepotism or favouritism and discrimination in recruitment, selection, performance evaluation, and promotion. It does not take too long before the organization experiences the dysfunctional effects of these practices. For example, the development among employees; the belief that rewards and outcomes, generally, are not contingent upon performance; and the even more serious consequence of employees experiencing feelings of powerlessness which invariably results in employee alienation (Kanungo, 1990). The problems faced by the leaders in such situations are: (a) how to bring about the integration of organizational members who belong to various kinship or social groups; and, (b) how to reduce worker alienation.

The problem of integration can be resolved by the use of a family metaphor for organizations – 'this company is one big family in which we are responsible for each other'. In addition, embeddedness can be enhanced through opportunities for active participation and team work. Of course, the foundation for these efforts is to ensure the process of open communications. The problem of work alienation can be reduced by the idealization of organizational and work values, through organizational socialization practices, and by setting up performance-contingent reward systems. A sense of belonging to an organization as a family is created among followers when they find that the leader is: (a) impartial – that is, fair and firm; (b) open, available and accessible; (c) concerned with improving their quality of work life; (d) sociable and collegial with them and their families; and, (e) respectful and supportive of the authority and position of others, particularly those in the second line positions of executive succession (Singh and Bhandarkar, 1990).

The leader has to act as a role model and set examples through deeds and actions to demonstrate his or her desire and interest in integrating all employees as members of the 'one' organization. A recent study of chief executives of five Indian organizations (Singh and Bhandarkar, 1990) supports the contention that the strategies of using the family metaphor 'Kutumbization' (that is, one undivided community) and empowerment techniques are the key to successful organizational transformation. A list of behaviours necessary for charismatic leadership effectiveness in developing countries, consistent with the preceding discussion, is presented in Table 6.1.

Table 6.1 Charismatic leadership behaviour for developing countries

1. Assess the Environment:
   - Identify factors that facilitate or hinder achievement of organizational goals
   - Assess minimum conditions needed for implementing short and long term goals
   - Prepare a stakeholder transaction matrix
2. Visioning and Responding to Environment:
   - Establish dominant goal and direct efforts to achieve it
   - Move from pilot testing to implementation on a larger scale
   - Mobilize demand
   - Develop support network
3. Means to Achieve:
   - Establish affective reciprocity relationship
     - confidence in follower's ability for task accomplishment
     - nurturing follower self efficacy through coaching, modelling, encouraging and rewarding
     - idealizing organizational and work values
   - Discourage manipulative ingratiation relationships
     - avoid lording behaviour and 'pulling of ranks'
     - avoid negativism
     - avoid favouritism
   - Promote performance based reward system
   - Promote loyalty to organization and work values rather than loyalty to people in position power
   - Recognize dependence of subordinates for developing task competence versus dependence for materials gain. Be supportive of subordinates in the former case
   - Use a family metaphor for organizations
     - be fair and firm to all members
     - be open, available and accessible
     - be sociable and collegial to members (use existing rites and rituals as occasions for relating to members)
     - show constant concern for improving quality of life of members as one would do for own self
     - groom second line in command
     - show respect and support for other's position and authority
     - promote information sharing, participation and communication

Finally, religious traditionalism noticed in many developing countries may operate as a cultural contingency variable for charismatic leadership effectiveness. The religious traditions in these countries are highly valued and often determine a leader's judgement of what path of action is morally right or wrong in a given situation. Such judgements have a strong influence in guiding the leader's behaviour. The influence of traditional religions and moral norms such as a concern for altruism, high femininity or caring and affiliative concerns, and low masculinity or competitive and acquisitive concerns are often considered to be inimical to the business interests of organizations (Weber, 1958b; Hofstede, 1980; Kanungo and Conger, 1990).

It is argued that the tendency of leaders in developing countries to be guided by moral rather than by pragmatic business considerations has a detrimental effect on public and private sector organizations, chiefly because it ignores or neglects the organization's objectives. This argument, however, is not entirely valid, and indeed highly questionable. Many leaders in developing countries were effective primarily because of their ability to integrate traditional religious and moral values with practical considerations for achieving the future goals of their organizations (Woycke, 1990). Even in Western industrialized countries, it is becoming increasingly evident that organizational leadership needs to have a moral and spiritual base (Kanungo and Conger, 1990; Kanungo and Mendonca, 1994) because without an ethical and altruistic perspective, the very survival of the business over the long term is in serious jeopardy.

Therefore, in order to be effective, charismatic leaders in developing countries need to provide moral leadership by integrating traditional religious values with pragmatic considerations. The traditional values can be incorporated in the idealization and articulation of future visions or goals. Furthermore, since these values are cherished by the people at large, the leader's commitment to and practice of these values would have two desirable effects. The first is that the leader's espousal of these values contributes to a greater follower acceptance of the leader's vision. The second effect that results when the leader lives and leads by these values is the followers' perception of congruence between what is espoused and practiced by the leader. As a result, the leader's credibility is greatly enhanced and, equally important, the leader serves as a role model for the followers.

In their study of transformational corporate leaders in India, Singh and Bhandarkar (1990) concluded thus: 'A dramatic illustration of this cultural imperative in recent times is Mahatma Gandhi who could unify and organize the diverse masses. Living by ideals is thus the value which is most cherished by people at large, and they desire to see these values more in their leaders, although they themselves may not necessarily practice them. In order to take care of the above, the change process must be characterized by role modelling, sincerity, and commitment on the part of the top management, and consistency between precept and practice' (p. 317).

It is recognized that religious traditionalism may create two opposite sets of belief or value systems that form the basis of desirable behaviours in some leaders, and undesirable behaviours in other leaders. Thus, in some leaders it may create a system of beliefs that includes beliefs in: heterogeneity and inequality among people – such as the belief in the caste and clan systems, and the 'we-and they-groups'; and an external locus of control, fatalism and destiny – for example, as influenced by the doctrine of *Karma* practiced in India. Other possible beliefs might include a preoccupation with the past or the absence of a futuristic orientation, or a sense of time being eternal or ever-present and never passing. Such beliefs make the leader ineffective in achieving organizational objectives. A leader who believes in 'inequality' often engages in patronage, favouritism and discrimination (Virmani and Guptam, 1991). Fatalism and the lack of a futuristic orientation make the leader incapable of visioning and planning to achieve task goals within targeted time periods.

Although such dysfunctional effects can be observed in some leaders, there are other leaders in whom the same religious traditionalism is seen to produce an opposite set of beliefs that have positive effects. Influenced by traditionalism, these leaders develop a system of beliefs emphasizing (as all religions do) heterogeneity and equality among people; internal self-control as they cope with environmental demands, which is also an element of the *Karma* doctrine that requires one to be responsible for one's actions; and a healthy optimism for the future. Leaders in non-Western cultures who interpret religious traditionalism in this way tend to implement more effectively the transformational strategies of idealizing the future vision, exercising moral influence, becoming role models, and empowering followers.

Besides such cultural contingencies for leadership effectiveness as described above, recent research work by House and his associates (House et al., 1999) testifies to the fact that charismatic/transformational leaders who exert moral influence are also perceived to possess several attributes and behavioural qualities that are universal across Western and non-Western cultures. In their Global Leadership and Organizational Effectiveness (GLOBE) Research Program involving 61 cultures throughout the world, they identified a number of universal and culturally contingent leadership attributes and behaviours contributing to leadership effectiveness. The project results found that: charismatic/value based leadership and team-oriented leadership were universally endorsed as contributing to outstanding leadership. The components of the charismatic/value based dimension are: charismatic (visionary, inspirational, self-sacrifice); integrity; decisive; performance oriented. In this category, three of the positively endorsed items relate to integrity – the leaders are seen as trustworthy, just, and honest. The components of the team-oriented dimension are: collaborative team orientation; team integrator; diplomatic, malevolent (reverse scored); administratively competent. On the other hand, leader characteristics such as being self-protective, malevolent, and face saver, were universally viewed as being impediments to leader effectiveness (House et al., 1999). 'The portrait of a leader who is universally viewed as effective is clear: the person should exhibit the integrity and charismatic qualities ... and build effective teams' (House et al., 1999, p.48).

Ethics of leadership motivation and influence processes: congruence with non-Western cultural norms and values

The discussion of the ethical dimensions in leadership motivation and leadership influence processes strongly argued that the nature, characteristics, and leader behaviours of the transformational mode of leadership are consistent with the altruistic ethic. The question that arises when we consider the cultural contingencies of leadership is whether the cultural norms and values that prevail in non-Western societies are compatible with the moral values that are inherent in the altruistic ethic. To address this question, we first draw some lessons from the cross-cultural studies in leadership discussed in this chapter. We then explore the values inherent in the basic religions and moral paradigms that are dominant in non-Western societies. Such an exploration is necessary because in traditional societies, these paradigms have been, and still are, the major forces that pervade the socialization of societal members; influence their norms, orientations, and behaviours; and help to explain the social institutions and structures.

The cross-cultural studies (Sinha, 1990; Mendonca and Kanungo, 1994), which explicitly used cultural variables to examine leader effectiveness, suggest that the task, social, and participative leader roles are effective in non-Western societies only to the extent that the roles are performed in the nurturant-task leadership mode. Now, the task, social, and participative leaders, as discussed in Chapter 4, use mainly the transactional influence process. But the focus of the nurturant-task leader is the growth and development of both the followers and the leader. The nurturant-task leadership model postulates that subordinates can be developed to a state of preparedness in order to function autonomously. This 'other' focus implies the use of the transformational influence process and, in that sense, the nurturant-task leadership model reflects the altruistic ethic. However, the nurturant-task model recognizes that as it succeeds in developing subordinates to become autonomous, it might, at the same time, cause the leader to resort to the transactional influence process and related control strategies because of the leader's fear that without his or her direction and control, productivity would be compromised. This focus on others of the nurturant-task leader would seem to be purely instrumental in attaining the leader's objective, and for this reason, it would tend to reflect more of the utilitarian or mutual altruism, rather than moral altruism.

Nevertheless, cross-cultural studies show that the task, social, and participative leader roles and the related transactional influence process are inappropriate, and the nurturant-task leader role is appropriate for non-Western cultures. These findings suggest two reasonable inferences. First, the egotistic values implicit in the control strategies of transactional leadership are generally incongruent with the cultural norms and values of these cultures. Second, the altruistic values, although of the utilitarian type, implicit in the development strategies of nurturant-task leadership, are congruent with the cultural norms and values of non-Western cultures.

However, the congruence of moral altruism with the cultural norms and values of non-Western cultures is much more clearly and convincingly demonstrated by the discussion, in the preceding section, of the culture fit of charismatic leadership. It will be noted from that discussion that the charismatic leader's empowering strategies, which reflect the altruistic values and ethics, can be implemented in a manner that is effective and, at the same time, consistent with the moral and ethical values in non-Western cultures, which are briefly presented in the next section.

From ancient times, people have turned to religion to understand the human condition and to seek answers to questions such as:

> What is a man? What is the meaning and purpose of our life? What is goodness and what is sin? What gives rise to our sorrows and to what intent? Where lies the path to true happiness? What is the truth about death, judgement, and retribution beyond the grave? What, finally, is that ultimate and unutterable mystery which engulfs our being, and whence we take our rise, and wither our journey leads us?
> (Second Vatican Council, 1965: 661)

Although the major religions that have shaped the cultural norms and values of non-Western societies might have different and even contradictory theological insights and responses to these questions, there is a remarkable consensus on the ethics of human behaviour. It would seem as if the norms of moral behaviour are deeply ingrained in human nature. And the underlying thrust of such norms is that the individual's growth and development comes about not when the individual seeks his or her own interests, but rather when the individual strives, even at great pain, risk, or inconvenience to the individual, to seek the good of the other-whether that other be a friend or foe or stranger.

In India, the Hindu way of life exhorts individuals to view themselves as instruments of the divine will, born to engage in moral duties that benefit the social order at the cost of considerable personal sacrifice (Buck, 1978). According to the Vedanta, the most influential school of Hindu thought, the ideal life is a process of growing to be nonegotistic, equananimous, stable-minded persons (Srinivas, 1994). The *Bhagavad Gita*, a holy scripture of Hinduism, advocates *Karmayoga* – the fulfilment of one's social duties and obligations with selfless detachment. The work of Chakraborty (1989a, 1989b) argues that *karmayoga* can form the basis of motivation of organizational leaders. Singh and Bhandarkar (1990) have shown the organizational leaders in India often act as *Karta* in the *Kutumba* context – as the father's role in the family, and the benevolent *Karta* role results in organizational transformation. Inherent in the *Karta* role is the altruistic intent; such a leadership role is ethical in nature.

Some empirical studies on values in India (Rani, 1969; Sinha, 1972) have shown that self-control, benevolence, and self-sacrifice are considered highly desirable values; and selfishness, greed, and attachment to sensual pleasures are considered undesirable values. Such value preferences are conducive to the practice of ethical leadership in India. These values and practices are embedded in the purpose of human life which, in the ancient Indian cultural tradition, is '... securing the emancipation of one's soul through the welfare of the world (*atmano mokshartham jagat hitayacha*). In other words, the concept that has been cherished through the long existence is the concept of welfare of all human beings (*lokasamgraha*) the welfare of the many and the happiness of the many (*bahujana sukhaya bahujana hitayacha*)' (Bhatta, 2002, p. 43).

Similar expressions of the altruistic ideal are found in Islam. For example, some of the deeply cherished values of Arab society are 'commitments to honour, honesty, respect to parents and older persons, loyalty to primary group, hospitality and generosity' (Ali and Azim, 1994). One of the five pillars of Islam is charity which signifies helping others and incorporates the values of honesty, charity, and service to others. In Sufism, described as the mystical core of Islam, the ultimate goal is to attain a state of self-realization. Sufism offers a detailed code of conduct for social relationships and discusses the duties and responsibilities towards friends and disciples (al-Ghazzali, 1966, 1975). The altruistic motivation inherent in these values clearly suggest that in Islam and Sufism one's personal goals and interests ought not to be pursued to the detriment of the goals and interests of the group or community.

The concept of the more inclusive self – that is, one in which the desires of the individual are subordinated to the needs of the larger community, is also found in Buddhism and Confucianism. Ethical conduct, universal love, and compassion are fundamentals of Buddhist teaching and practices. A person who is in a position of leadership and authority is required to live according to the following ten principles: generosity, morality, self-sacrifice, honesty, kindness, austerity or self-control, non-anger, non-violence or non-oppression, patience, and living in accord with Dharma (truth). Thus, one Buddhist sect is known to emphasize personal sacrifice and service to others (Smart, 1983). In a similar vein, Confucianism depicts individuals as embedded in a larger social order with a set of obligations to define themselves in relation to others and to foster harmony in their relations (Tuan, 1982; Ho, 1985).

The knowledge that society's well-being ought to supersede one's own well-being is inherent in the nature of human beings, but its development is affected by the socialization process. In this process, the individuals' spiritual experiences that stem from their religious beliefs and practices serve to further reinforce altruistic behaviour. Therefore, the religious influences that characterize non-Western societies will serve to hinder the effectiveness of the transactional leadership mode and facilitate the effectiveness of the transformational leadership mode. 'Am I my brother's keeper?' This question explicitly raised in: the Judeo-Christian scriptures, is also echoed in the scriptures and literature of other religious and cultural traditions. Indeed, in every age and in every culture, the tapestry of human life and living is greatly enriched and made more vibrant by the thread of concern for others before concern for one's self. It is, therefore, not surprising that leaders whose lives have left a profound, beneficial influence on their followers – in their own day and today continue to be models for others to emulate – are those who have been true to the noble ideal so well expressed by John Ruskin: 'That man is richest who, having perfected the functions of his own life to the utmost, has also the widest helpful influence, both personal, and by means of his possessions, over the lives of others' (quoted in Bartlett, 1968, p. 698).

Conclusion

The major thrust of the discussion in this chapter was to examine the culture fit of the four major leadership roles relative to the sociocultural characteristics of developing countries and the internal work culture of organizations in these countries. We discussed the impact of cultural contingencies on the effectiveness of each role. However, keeping in mind that bringing about change or coping with change is *the* dominant and urgent need for organizations in developing countries, the charismatic leadership role emerged as the most appropriate and critical for organizational leaders in these countries. Organizational change is the essence of development. Hence, organizations in developing countries need change more than the maintenance of the status quo.

Bringing about effective changes requires the initiative, guidance, and effort of charismatic leaders – particularly in the development of appropriate strategies on three fronts: (a) an environmental assessment, (b) visioning and responding to the complexities of the environment, and (c) member ingratiation using a family metaphor and member empowerment to achieve organizational goals. The chapter considered the cultural variables that are derived from authoritarianism, collectivism, and traditionalism and that might facilitate or hinder these efforts and proposed specific strategies to build on the cultural facilitators and overcome the cultural constraints.

The chapter also examined the norms and values that pervade the developing non-Western societies and concluded that these are congruent with the altruistic ethic that underlies the transformational leadership process.

Suggested questions for reflection

- What are the major dimensions of cultures in non-Western societies?
- What is the impact of the cultural dimensions on the task, social, and participative leader roles?
- What is the impact of culture on the charismatic leader role?
- Do Western and non-Western societies agree on the components of the ethics of human behaviour?
- Can the norms of moral behaviour be considered ingrained in human nature?

Appendix I
Items in the Conger-Kanungo
Charismatic Leadership Scale

Sensitivity to the environment (SE)

Readily recognizes constraints in the physical environment (technological limitations, lack of resources, etc.) that may stand in the way of achieving organizational objectives.

Readily recognizes constraints in the organization's social and cultural environment (cultural norms, lack of grass roots support, etc.) that may stand in the way of achieving organizational objectives.

Recognizes the limitations of other members of the organization.

Recognizes the abilities and skills of other members of the organization.

Sensitivity to member needs (SMN)

Shows sensitivity for the needs and feelings of the other members in the organization.

Influences others by developing mutual liking and respect.

Often expresses personal concern for the needs and feelings of other members in the organization.

Strategic vision and articulation (SVA)

Provides inspiring strategic and organizational goals.

Inspirational; able to motivate by articulating effectively the importance of what organizational members are doing.

Consistently generates new ideas for the future of the organization.

Exciting public speaker.

Has vision; often brings up ideas about possibilities for the future.

Entrepreneurial; seizes new opportunities in order to achieve goals.

Readily recognizes new environmental opportunities (favourable physical and social conditions) that may facilitate achievement of organizational objectives.

Personal risk (PR)

Takes high personal risks for the sake of the organization.

Often incurs high personal cost for the good of the organization.

In pursuing organizational objectives, engages in activities involving considerable personal risk.

Unconventional behaviour (UB)

Engages in unconventional behaviour in order to achieve organizational goals.

Uses non-traditional means to achieve organizational goals.

Often exhibits very unique behaviour that surprises other members of the organization.

Appendix II
Items in the Kanungo-Menon Managerial Resourcefulness Scale

Goal Directed Problem Orientation (GDPO)

1. When a colleague discusses his/her problem, I steer the conversation to something else.
2. While doing a task, I sometimes lose sight of my goals.
3. I think it is necessary to use formal authority positions to get others to do what I want.
4. When I am not sure I can successfully handle a task, I tend to avoid it.
5. I do not like people who are too particular about getting things done on time.
6. I do not care much for details.
7. I do not spend time looking to see how the present situation is similar to past situations.
8. I find criticism directed towards me annoying and often wish people would keep their opinions to themselves.
9. When someone interferes with my task, I get angry with him/her.

Proactive Analytical Orientation (PAO)

1. When faced with a disturbing problem, I concentrate on what I need to do, instead of getting upset.
2. I always make an effort to analyse the components of the goal to be achieved.
3. I tend to analyse the reasons for my successes or failures.
4. Information gathering is part of my initial problem-solving techniques.
5. I share what I know.

6. I like people who would say 'I can do it' when faced with difficult tasks.
7. Generally, I tend to get involved to understand other's problems.

Problem Focused Perseverance (PFP)

1. When I find a task too difficult, I have a tendency to put it off or delay it through time-consuming activities such as taking a drink/ snack/cigarette/or conversing with a colleague.
2. I tend to stop/hesitate doing a job when major difficulties come in the way.
3. In dealing with a task, I have a general notion of what I would do but not the precise action plans.
4. While doing a job, if a more interesting job appears on my table, I tend to switch to the latter.

Emotional Equanimity (EE)

1. When close to a deadline and I have not finished/prepared for the meeting/presentation, I become so nervous and anxious about the upcoming deadline that I find it difficult to concentrate.
2. When faced with a new problem situation, I often get swept away by my emotions and find it difficult to concentrate.
3. Often I cannot control my excitement when I am close to being successful in what I am doing.
4. I get too depressed with personal failure.

References

Abramson, L. Y., Garber, J. and Seligman, M. E. P. (1980) Learned helplessness in humans: an attributional analysis, in J. Garber and M. E. P. Seligman (eds), *Human Helplessness: Theory and Applications*, pp. 3–34. New York: Academic Press.

Adler, M. J. (1981) *Six Great Ideas*. New York: Macmillan.

Al-Ghazzali (1966) *The Book of Knowledge*, trans N.A. Faris. Lahore: Muhammad Ashraf.

Al-Ghazzali (1975) *On the Duties of Brotherhood*, trans M. Holland. London: Latimer.

Ali, J. A. and Azim, A. (1994) *Islamic Work Ethic and Organizational Development*. Paper presented at the 23rd International Congress of Applied Psychology, Madrid, Spain, July.

Andrews, K. R. (1989) Ethics in practice, *Harvard Business Review*, September–October: 99–104.

Andriessen, E. J. H. and Drenth, P. J. D. (1984) Leadership: theories and models, in P. J. D. Drenth, H. Thierry, P. J. Willems and C. J. de Wolff (eds), *Handbook of Work and Organizational Psychology*, pp. 481–520. New York: John Wiley.

Avolio, B. J. and Bass, B. M. (1988) Transformational leadership, charisma, and beyond, in J. G. Hunt, B. R. Baliga, H. P. Dachler and C. A. Schriesheim (eds), *Emerging Leadership Vistas*, pp. 29–49. Lexington, MA: D. C. Heath.

Bakan, D. (1966) *The Duality of Human Existence*. Chicago: Rand McNally.

Bales, R. F. and Slater, P. E. (1955) Role differentiation in small decision-making groups, in T. Parson and R. F. Bales (eds), *Family, Socialization, and Interaction Process*, pp. 259–306. Glencoe, IL: Free Press.

Bandura, A. (1977) Self-efficacy: toward a unifying theory of behavioral change, *Psychological Review*, 84: 191–215.

Bandura, A. (1986) *Social Foundations of Thought and Action: A Social-Cognitive View*. Englewood Cliffs, NJ: Prentice Hall.

Bartlett, J. (1968) *Familiar Quotations: A Collection of Passages, Phrases, and Proverbs Traced to their Sources in Ancient and Modern Literature*. Boston: Little, Brown.

Bass, B. M. (1985) *Leadership Performance Beyond Expectations*. New York: Academic Press.

Bass, B. M. (1990) *Bass and Stogdill's Handbook of Leadership*, 3rd edn. New York: Free Press.

Bass, B. M. and Avolio, B. J. (1993) Transformational leadership: a response to critiques, in M. Chemers and R. Ayman (eds), *Leadership Theory and Research: Perspectives and Directions*, pp. 49–80. San Diego: Academic Press.

Bass, B. M. and Burger, P. C. (1979) *Assessment of Managers: An International Comparison.* New York: Free Press.

Bass, B. M. and Steidlmeier, P. (2004) Ethics, character, and authentic transformational leadership behavior, in J. B. Ciulla (ed.), *Ethics, the Heart of Leadership*, pp.175–96. Westport, CT: Praeger.

Baumeister, R. (1987) How the self became a problem: a psychological review of historical research, *Journal of Personality and Social Psychology*, 52: 163–76.

Beckhard, R. (1996) On future leaders, in F. Heselbeib, M. Goldsmith and R. Beckhard (eds), *The Leader of the Future: New Visions, Strategies, and Practices for the Next Era*, pp. 125–9. San Francisco: Jossey-Bass.

Bennis, W. G. and Nanus, B. (1985) *Leaders.* New York: Harper & Row.

Berenbeim, R. E. (1987) *Corporate Ethics.* New York: Conference Board, Inc.

Berkowitz, L. (1972) Social norms, feelings, and other factors affecting helping and altruism, in L. Berkowitz (ed.), *Advances in Experimental Psychology*, pp. 63–108. New York: Academic Press.

Berlew, D. E. (1974) Leadership and organizational excitement, *California Management Review*, 17: 21–30.

Bettelheim, B. (1943) Individual and mass behavior in extreme situations, *Journal of Abnormal and Social Psychology*, 38: 417–52.

Bhatta, C. Panduranga (2002) Positive action: cultural insights into motivation, *Global Business Review*, 3(1): 39–52.

Blake, R. R. and Mouton, J. S. (1964) *The Managerial Grid.* Houston: Gulf.

Blanchard, K. and Peale, N. V. (1988) *The Power of Ethical Management.* New York: Fawcett Crest.

Blau, P. M. (1974) *Exchange and Power in Social Life.* New York: John Wiley.

Blauner, R. (1964) *Alienation and Freedom.* Chicago: University of Chicago Press.

Block, P. (1987) *The Empowered Manager.* San Francisco: Jossey-Bass.

Bond, M. H. and Hwang, K. K. (1986) The social psychology of Chinese people, in M. H. Bond (ed.), *The Psychology of the Chinese People*, pp. 213–66. Hong Kong: Oxford University Press.

Bowie, N. E. (1998) A Kantian theory of meaningful work, *Journal of Business Ethics*, 17: 1083–92.

Boyatzis, R. E. (1982) *The Competent Manager: A Model for Effective Performance.* New York: John Wiley.

Boyatzis, R. E. (1984) The need for close relationships and the manager's job, in D. A. Kolb, I. M. Rubin and J. M. McIntyre (eds), *Organizational Psychology: Readings on Human Behavior in Organizations*, pp. 81–6. Englewood Cliffs, NJ: Prentice Hall.

Braden, W. (1970) *The Age of Aquarius.* Chicago: Quadrangle Books.

Bradley, R. T. (1987) *Charisma and Social Structure: A Study of Love and Power, Wholeness and Transformation.* New York: Paragon.

Brief, A.P., Dukerich, J.M., Brown, P.R. and Brett, J.F. (1996) What's wrong with the Treadway Commission Report?, *Journal of Business Ethics*, 15(2): 183–98.

Brief, A. P. and Motowidlo, S. J. (1986) Prosocial organizational behaviors, *Academy of Management Review*, 11: 710–25.

Bryman, A. (1986) *Leadership and Organizations*. London: Routledge & Kegan Paul.

Buck, W. (1978) *Ramayana*. New York: New American Library.

Burke, W. (1986) Leadership as empowering others, in S. Srivastva et al., *Executive Power: How Executives Influence People and Organizations*. San Francisco: Jossey-Bass.

Burns, J. M. (1978) *Leadership*. New York: Harper & Row.

Bynner, W. (1962) *The Way of Life According to Lao Tzu*. New York: Capricorn.

Campbell, D. (1975) On the conflicts between biological and social evolution and between psychology and moral tradition, *American Psychologist*, 30: 1103–26.

Cartwright, D. (1965) Leadership, influence and control, in J. G. March (ed.), *Handbook of Organizations*, pp. 1–47. Chicago: Rand McNally.

Cartwright, D. and Zander, A. (eds) (1968) *Group Dynamics: Research and Theory*. New York: Harper & Row.

Chakraborty, S. K. (1989a) Values for Indian managers: what and where to seek, *Decision*, 16(3): 177.

Chakraborty, S. K. (1989b) *Foundations of Managerial Work: Contributions from Indian Thought*. Bombay: Himalaya Publishing House.

Chaput, C. (2002) Renewing our public life, *http://www.zenit.org*, accessed 10 October.

Colvin, G. (2003) Corporate crooks are not all created equal, *Fortune*, October, 27: 64.

Concise Oxford English Dictionary of Current English (1964) 5th edn. London: Oxford University Press.

Conger, J. A. (1985) *Charismatic Leadership in Business: An Exploratory Study*. Unpublished doctoral dissertation, Harvard University, School of Business Administration.

Conger, J. A. (1989) *The Charismatic Leader*. San Francisco: Jossey-Bass.

Conger, J. A. and Kanungo, R. N. (1987) Toward a behavioral theory of charismatic leadership in organizational settings, *Academy of Management Review*, 12: 637–47.

Conger, J. A. and Kanungo, R. N. (1988a) Behavioral dimensions of charismatic leadership, in J. A. Conger and R. N. Kanungo (eds), *Charismatic Leadership: The Elusive Factor in Organizational Effectiveness*, pp. 78–97. San Francisco: Jossey-Bass.

Conger, J. A. and Kanungo, R. N. (eds) (1988b) *Charismatic Leadership: The Elusive Factor in Organizational Effectiveness*. San Francisco: Jossey-Bass.

Conger, J. A. and Kanungo, R. N. (1988c) The empowerment process: integrating theory and practice, *Academy of Management Review*, 13: 471–82.

Conger, J. A. and Kanungo, R. N. (1988d) Patterns and trends in studying charismatic leadership, in I. A. Conger and R. N. Kanungo (eds), *Charismatic Leadership: The Elusive Factor in Organizational Effectiveness*, pp. 324–36. San Francisco: Jossey-Bass.

Conger, J. A. and Kanungo, R. N. (1992) Perceived behavioral attributes of charismatic leadership, *Canadian Journal of Behavioral Sciences*, 24: 86–102.

Conger, J. A. and Kanungo, R. N. (1994) Charismatic leadership in organizations: perceived behavioral attributes and their measurement, *Journal of Organizational Behavior*, 15: 439–52.

Conger, J. A. and Kanungo, R. N. (1998) *Charismatic Leadership in Organizations*. Thousand Oaks, CA: Sage Publications.

Conger, J. A., Kanungo, R. N., Menon, S. T. and Mathur, P. (1997) Measuring charisma: dimensionality and validity of the Conger-Kanungo scale of charismatic leadership, *Canadian Journal of Administrative Sciences*, 14(3): 290–302.

Conger, J. A., Kanungo, R. N. and Menon, S. T. (2000) Charismatic leadership and follower effects, *Journal of Organizational Behavior*, 21: 747–67.

Cowley, W. H. (1928) Three distinctions in the study of leaders, *Journal of Abnormal and Social Psychology*, 23: 144–57.

Daboub, A. I., Rasheed, A. M. A., Priem, R. L. and Gray, D. A. (1995) Top management team characteristics and corporate illegal activity, *Academy of Management Review*, 20: 138–70.

Dahl, R. A. (1957) The concept of power, *Behavioral Science*, 2: 201–18.

Dawes, R. (1975) Formal models of dilemmas in social-decision making, in M. Kaplan and S. Schwartz (eds), *Human Judgment and Decision Processes*. New York: Academic Press.

Deci, E. L. (1975) *Intrinsic Motivation*. New York: Plenum.

Deutsch, M. (1973) *The Resolution of Conflict: Constructive and Destructive Processes*. New Haven, CT: Yale University Press.

Dorfman, P. W. (1994) *Cross Cultural Leadership Research: Issues and Assumptions*. Paper presented at the SIDP conference symposium, Nashville, TN, April.

Dow, T. E. (1969) A theory of charisma, *Social Quarterly*, 10: 306–18.

Drucker, P. F. (1968) *The Practice of Management*. London: Pan Books.

Dyer, W. (1977) *Team Building*. Reading, MA: Addison-Wesley.

Earley, P. C. (1993) East meets West meets Mideast: further explorations of collectivistic and individualistic work groups, *Academy of Management Journal*, 36: 319–48.

Eden, D. (1990) Industrialization as a self-fulfilling prophecy: the role of expectations in development, *International Journal of Psychology*, 25: 871–86.

Emerson, R. M. (1962) Power-dependence relations, *American Sociological Review*, 27: 31–41.

Erez, M. (1994) Toward a model of cross-cultural industrial and organizational psychology, in H. C. Triandis, M. D. Dunnette and L. M. Hough (eds), *Handbook of Industrial and Organizational Psychology*, Vol. 4, pp. 559–608. Palo Alto, CA: Consulting Psychologists Press.

Etzioni, A. (1989) Money, power, and fame, *Newsweek*, 18 September: 10.

Evans, M. G. (1970) The effects of supervisory behavior on the path-goal relationship, *Organizational Behavior and Human Performance*, 5: 277–98.

Fiedler, F. E. (1967) *A Theory of Leadership Effectiveness*. New York: McGraw-Hill.

Fiedler, F. E. and Chemers, M. M. (1984) *Improving Leadership Effectiveness: The Leader-Match Concept*. New York: Wiley.

Finlay, J. R. (1995) Business ethics is not a soft issue, it's a matter of survival, *The Financial Post* (Canada), 11 March: 21.

Fleishman, E. A., Harris, E. F. and Burtt, H. E. (1955) *Leadership and Supervision in Industry*. Columbus: Ohio State University, Bureau of Educational Research.

French, J. R. P., Jr and Raven, B. (1959) The bases of social power, in D. P. Cartwright (ed.), *Studies in Social Power*, pp. 150–67. Ann Arbor, MI: Institute for Social Research.

Friedland, W. H. (1964) For a sociological concept of charisma, *Social Forces*, 43: 18–26.

Friedman, M. (1963) *Capitalism and Freedom*. Chicago: University of Chicago Press.

Galbraith, J. (1967) *The New Industrial State*. Boston: Houghton Mifflin.

George, J. M. and Brief, A. P. (1992) Feeling good, going good: a conceptual analysis of the mood at work-organizational spontaneity relationship, *Psychological Bulletin*, 112: 310–29.

Gould, A. (2005) Development requires virtue, says Nobel Peace Prize Winner. *http://www.mercatornet.com*, p. 2.

Gouldner, A. (1960) The norm of reciprocity: a preliminary statement, *American Sociological Review*, 25: 161–78.

Growald, E. and Luks, A. (1988) Beyond self, *American Health*, 7: 51–3.

Haire, M., Ghiselli, E. F. and Porter, L. W. (1966) *Managerial Thinking: An International Study*. New York: John Wiley.

Halcrow, A. (1987) Outlook: is there a crisis in business ethics? *Personnel Journal*, November: 10–17.

Halpin, A. W. and Winer, B. J. (1957) A factorial study of the leader behaviour descriptions, in R. M. Stoddill and A. E. Coons (eds), *Leader Behaviour: Its Description and Measurement*. Columbus: Ohio State University, Bureau of Business Research.

Hardin, G. (1968) The tragedy of the commons, *Science*, 162: 1243–8.

Hersey, P. and Blanchard, K. H. (1984) *The Management of Organizational Behaviour*. Englewood Cliffs, NJ: Prentice Hall.

Hirsch, F. (1976) *Social Limits to Growth*. Cambridge, MA: Harvard University Press.

Ho, D. (1985) Cultural values and professional issues in clinical psychology: implications from the Hong Kong experience, *American Psychologist*, 40: 1212–18.

Hofstede, G. (1980) *Culture's Consequences: International Differences in Work-Related Values*. Beverly Hills, CA: Sage.

Hofstede, G. (1993) Cultural constraints in management theories, *The Executive*, 7: 81–94.

Hogan, R., Curphy, G. J. and Hogan, J. (1994) What we know about leadership: effectiveness and personality, *American Psychologist*, 49: 493–504.

Hollander, E. P. (1958) Conformity, status, and idiosyncrasy credit, *Psychological Review*, 65: 117–27.

Hollander, E. P. (1978) *Leadership Dynamics*. New York: Free Press.

Hollander, E. P. (1979) Leadership and social exchange processes, in K. Gergen, M. S. Greenberg and R. H. Willis (eds), *Social Exchange: Advances in Theory and Research*, pp. 103–18. New York: Winston-Wiley.

Hollander, E. P. (1986) On the central role of leadership processes, *International Review of Applied Psychology*, 35: 39–52.

Hollander, E. P. and Offermann, L. R. (1990) Power and leadership in organizations, *American Psychologist*, 45: 179–89.

Homans, A. (1974). *Social Behavior: Its Elementary Forms*. New York: Harcourt Brace Jovanovich.

House, R. J. (1971) A path-goal theory of leadership effectiveness, *Administrative Science Quarterly*, 16: 321–32.

House, R. J. (1977) A 1976 theory of charismatic leadership, in J. G. Hunt and L. L. Larson (eds), *Leadership: The Cutting Edge*, pp. 189–207. Carbondale: Southern Illinois University Press.

House, R. J. (1988a) Leadership research: some forgotten, ignored, or overlooked findings, in J. G. Hunt, B. R. Baliga, H. P. Dachler and C. A. Schriesheim (eds), *Emerging Leadership Vistas*, pp. 245–60. Lexington, MA: D. C. Heath.

House, R. J. (1988b) Power and personality in complex organizations, in L. L. Cummings and B. M. Staw (eds), *Research in Organizational Behavior: An Annual Review of Critical Essays and Reviews*, Vol. 10, pp. 305–57. Greenwich, CF: JAI.

House, R. J. (1995) Leadership in the twenty-first century: a speculative inquiry, in A. Howard (ed.), *The Changing Nature of Work*, pp. 411–50. San Francisco: Jossey-Bass.

House, R. J. and Dessler, G. (1974) The path-goal theory of leadership: some post hoc and a priori tests, in J. G. Hunt and L. L. Larson (eds), *Contingency Approaches to Leadership*, pp. 29–55. Carbondale: Southern Illinois University Press.

House, R. J. and Mitchell, T. R. (1974) Path-goal theory of leadership, *Journal of Contemporary Business*, 3(4): 81–97.

House, R. J. and Singh, J. (1987) Organizational behavior: some new directions for 1/0 psychology, *Annual Review of Psychology*, 38: 669–718.

House, R. J., Spangler, W. D. and Woycke, J. (1991) Personality and charisma in the U.S. presidency: a psychological theory of leader effectiveness, *Administrative Science Quarterly*, 36: 364–96.

House, R. J., Woycke, J. and Fodor, E. (1988) Charismatic and noncharismatic leaders: differences in behavior and effectiveness, in J. A. Conger and R. N. Kanungo (eds), *Charismatic Leadership: The Elusive Factor in Organizational Effectiveness*, pp. 98–121. San Francisco: Jossey-Bass.

House, R. J., Hanges, P. J., Ruiz-Quintanilla, S. A., Dorfman, P. W., Javidan, M., Dickson, M., Gupta, V., et al. (1999) *Cultural Influences on Leadership and Organizations: Project GLOBE. http://leadership.wharton.upenn.edu/l_change/publications/house.shtml*

Hovland, C. I. and Pritzker, H. A. (1957) Extent of opinion change as a function of amount of change advocated, *Journal of Abnormal Psychology*, 54: 257–61.

Howell, J. M. (1988) Two faces of charisma, in J. A. Conger and R. N. Kanungo (eds), *Charismatic Leadership: The Elusive Factor in Organizational Effectiveness*, pp. 213–36. San Francisco: Jossey-Bass.

Howell, J. M. and Avolio, B. J. (1992) The ethics of charismatic leadership: submission or liberation? *Academy of Management Executive*, 6(2): 43–54.

Hunt, J. G. (1984) Organizational leadership: the contingency paradigm and its challenges, in B. Kellerman (ed.), *Leadership: Multidisciplinary Perspectives*, pp. 113–38. Englewood Cliffs, NJ: Prentice Hall.

Hunt, J. G. (1991) *Leadership: A New Synthesis*. Newbury Park, CA: Sage.

Hunt, J. G., Baliga, B. R., Dachler, H. P. and Schriesheim, C. A. (eds) (1988) *Emerging Leadership Vistas*. Lexington, MA: D.C. Heath.

Jackson, D. (1967) *Personality Research Form Manual*. Goshen, NY: Research Psychologists Press.

Jago, A. G., Reber, G., Bohnisch, W., Maczynski, J., Zavrel, J. and Dudorkin, J. (1993) *Culture's Consequence? A Seven Nation Study of Participation*. Paper presented at the meeting of the Decision Sciences Institute, Washington, DC, November.

Jenkins, C., Rosenman, R. and Zyzanski, S. (1974) Prediction of clinical coronary heart disease by a test for the coronary-prone behavior pattern, *New England Journal of Medicine*, 23: 1271–5.

John Paul II (1981) *Encyclical laborem exercens*. Ottawa, Ontario: Canadian Conference of Catholic Bishops.

John Paul II (1994) *Crossing the Threshold of Hope*. Toronto, Ontario: Knopf.

Kangas, E. A. (1988) Introduction, in *Ethics in American Business: A Special Report*, pp. 5–14. New York: Touche Ross.

Kanter, R. M. (1979) Power failure in management circuits, *Harvard Business Review*, July–August: 65–75.

Kanter, R. M. (1983) *The Change Masters*. New York: Simon & Schuster.

Kanungo, R. N. (1977) Bases of supervisory power and job satisfaction in bicultural context, in H. C. Jain and R. N. Kanungo (eds), *Behavioral Issues in Management: The Canadian Context*, pp. 331–44. Toronto: McGraw-Hill Ryerson.

Kanungo, R. N. (1982) *Work Alienation*. New York: Praeger.

Kanungo, R. N. (1987) Reward management: a new look, in S. Dolan and R. Schuler (eds), *Canadian Readings and Human Resource Management*, pp. 261–75. St Papl, MN: West.

Kanungo, R. N. (1990) Culture and work alienation: Western models and Eastern realities, *International Journal of Psychology*, 25: 795–812.

Kanungo, R. N. (2001) Ethical values of transactional and transformational leaders, *Canadian Journal of Administrative Sciences*, 18(4): 257–65.

Kanungo, R. N. and Conger, J. A. (1990) The quest for altruism in organizations, in S. Srivastva and D. L. Cooperrider (eds), *Appreciative Management and Leadership*, pp. 256–88. San Francisco: Jossey-Bass.

Kanungo, R. N. and Conger, J. (1993) Promoting altruism as a corporate goal, *Academy of Management Executive*, 7(3): 37–48.

Kanungo, R. N. and Jaeger, A. M. (1990) Introduction: the need for indigenous management in developing countries, in A. M. Jaeger and R. N. Kanungo (eds), *Management in Developing Countries*, pp. 1–19. London: Routledge.

Kanungo, R. N. and Mendonca, M. (1992) *Compensation: Effective Reward Management*. Toronto, Ontario: Butterworths.

Kanungo, R. N. and Mendonca, M. (1994) What leaders cannot do without: the spiritual dimensions of leadership, in J. A. Conger (ed.), *Spirit at Work*, pp. 162–98. San Francisco: Jossey-Bass.

Kanungo, R. N. and Mendonca, M. (1996a) Corporate leadership in the context of liberalization in India, *The Social Engineer*, 5(2): 114–36.

Kanungo, R. N. and Mendonca, M. (1996b) Cultural contingencies and leadership in developing countries, in P. A. Banberger, M. Erez and S. B. Bacharach (eds), *Research in the Sociology of Organizations*, pp. 263–95. Greenwich, CT: JAI Press.

Kanungo, R. N. and Mendonca, M. (1997a) *Fundamentals of Organizational Behaviour*. Dubuque, IA: Kendall/Hunt.

Kanungo, R. N. and Mendonca, M. (1997b) *Compensation: Effective Reward Management*, 2nd edn. Toronto, Ontario: John Wiley.

Kanungo, R. N. and Menon, S. T. (2005) Managerial resourcefulness: measuring a critical component of leadership effectiveness, *The Journal of Entrepreneurship*, 14(1): 39–55.

Kanungo, R. N. and Misra, S. (1992) Managerial resourcefulness: a reconceptualization of management skills, *Human Relations*, 45(12): 1311–32.

Katz, D. and Kahn, R. (1978) *The Social Psychology of Organizations*, 2nd edn. Toronto, Ontario: Wiley.

Kedia, B. L. and Bhagat, R. S. (1988) Cultural constraints on transfer of technology across nations: implications for research in international and comparative management, *Academy of Management Review*, 13: 559–71.

Kelman, H. C. (1958) Compliance, identification, and internalization: three processes of attitude change, *Journal of Conflict Resolution*, 2: 51–60.

Kenis, I. (1977) A cross-cultural study of personality and leadership, *Group and Organization Studies*, 2(1): 49–60.

Kerr, S. and Jermier, J. M. (1978) Substitutes for leadership: their meaning and measurement, *Organizational Behavior and Human Performance*, 22: 375–403.

Kets de Vries, M. F. R. (1994) The leadership mystique, *Academy of Management Executive*, 8(3): 73–89.

Kohlberg, L. (1969) Stage and sequence: a cognitive-developmental approach to socialization, in D. Goslin (ed.), *Handbook of Socialization Theory*, pp. 347–480. Chicago: Rand McNally.

Kramer, R. (1991) *Ed School Follies: The Miseducation of America's Teachers*. New York: Free Press.

Krebs, D. (1982) Altruism: a rational approach, in H. Eizenberg (ed.), *The Development of Prosocial Behavior*, pp. 53–76. New York: Academic Press.

Kreeft, P. (1990) *Making Choices: Practical Wisdom for Everyday Moral Decisions*. Ann Arbor, MI: Servant.

Kupczak, J. (2000) *Destined for Liberty: The Human Person in the Philosophy of Karol Wojtyla/John Paul II*. Washington, DC: The Catholic University of America Press.

Lank, A. G. (1988) The ethical criterion in business decision-making: optional or imperative? in *Ethics in American Business: A Special Report*, p. 47. New York: Touche Ross.

Lawler, E.E. (1973) *Motivation in Work Organizations*. Monterey, CA: Brooks/Cole.

Leavitt, H. (1986) *Corporate Pathfinders*. Homewood, IL: Dow Jones-Irwin.

Levinson, H. (1976) *Psychological Man*. Cambridge, MA: Levinson Institute.

Levitt, T. (1958) The dangers of social responsibility, *Harvard Business Review*, 36(5): 41–50.

Lewin, K., Lippitt, R. and White, R. K. (1939) Patterns of aggressive behavior in experimentally created social climates, *Journal of Social Psychology*, 10: 271–99.

Likert, R. (1961) *New Patterns of Management*. New York: McGraw-Hill.

Likert, R. (1967) *The Human Organization: Its Management and Value*. New York: McGraw-Hill.

Lippitt, R. and White, R. K. (1947) An experimental study of leadership and group life, in E. E. Maccoby, T. M. Newcomb and E. C. Hartley (eds), *Readings in Social Psychology*, pp. 496–511. New York: Holt, Rinehart & Winston.

Litwin, G. H. and Stringer, R. A., Jr (1968) *Motivation and Organizational Climate*. Boston: Harvard Business School, Division of Research.

Locke, E. A. and Latham, G. P. (1984) Goal setting: a motivational technique that works, *Organizational Dynamics*, 8(2): 68–80.

Loevinger, J. (1976) *Ego Development: Conceptions and Theories*. San Francisco: Jossey-Bass.

Luthans, F. and Kreitner, R. (1975) *Organizational Behavior Modification*. Glenview, IL: Scott Foresman.

Macaulay, J. and Berkowitz, L. (1970) Overview, in J. Macaulay and L. Berkowitz (eds), *Altruism and Helping Behavior*, pp. 1–12. New York: Academic Press.

Marcus, J. T. (1961) Transcendence and charisma, *Western Political Quarterly*, 14: 236–41.

Maslow, A. (1965) *Eupsychian Management*. Homewood, IL: Irwin.

Maslow, A. (1967) A theory of metamotivation: the biological rootings of the value life, *Journal of Humanistic Psychology*, 7: 108–9.

Maslow, A. (1973) Deficiency motivation and growth motivation, in D. C.

McClelland and R. S. Steele (eds), *Human Motivation: A Book of Readings*, pp. 233–51. Morristown, NJ: General Learning.

McClelland, D. C. (1961) *The Achieving Society*. Princeton, NJ: Van Nostrand.

McClelland, D. C. (1975) *Power: The Inner Experience*. New York: John Wiley.

McClelland, D. C. (1985). *Human Motivation*. Glenview, IL: Scott Foresman.

McClelland, D. C. and Burnham, D. H. (1995) Power is the great motivator, *Harvard Business Review*, January–February: 126–39.

McGregor, D. (1960) *The Human Side of Enterprise*. New York: McGraw-Hill.

McKenna, B. (2002) 'Bankruptcy of character' exposed at Enron congressional hearings, *Globe and Mail*, p. B8.

Mehta, P. (1994) Empowering the people for social achievement, in R. N. Kanungo and M. Mendonca (eds), *Work Motivation: Models for Developing Countries*, pp. 161–83. New Delhi: Sage.

Mehta, S. N. (2003) Is being good good enough? *Fortune*, 27 October: 117.

Meindl, J. R., Ehrlich, S. B. and Dukerich, J. M. (1985) The romance of leadership, *Administrative Science Quarterly*, 30: 78–102.

Mendonca, M. and Kanungo, R. N. (1994) Managing human resources: the issue of cultural fit, *Journal of Management Inquiry*, 3: 189–205.

Mendonca, M. (2001) Preparing for Ethical Leadership in Organizations, *Canadian Journal of Administrative Sciences, 18(4): 266: 276*.

Mensa chapter sparks furor (1995) *Globe and Mail*, 11 January, p. A6.

Merck & Co. (2000) 'The story of Mectizan' *http://www.merck.com/overview/philanthropy/mectizan/pl.htm*, accessed 9 May.

Mill, J. S. (1967) Utilitarianism, in E. A. Burtt (ed.) *The English Philosophers from Bacon to Mill*, pp. 895–948. New York: Modern Library.

Mintzberg, H. (1982) A note on that dirty word, 'efficiency', *Interfaces*, 12(5): 101–5.

Mintzberg, H. (1983) *Power in and around Organizations*. Englewood Cliffs, NJ: Prentice Hall.

Misumi, J. (1985) *The Behavioral Science of Leadership: An Interdisciplinary Japanese Research Program*. Ann Arbor: University of Michigan Press.

Misumi, J. (1988) *The Meaning of Work (MOW) for the Japanese and Action Research on Small Group Activities in Japanese Industrial Organizations*. Paper presented at the International Symposium on Social Values and Effective Organizations, Taipei, Taiwan, November.

Misumi, J. and Peterson, M. F. (1985) The performance-maintenance (PM) theory of leadership: review of a Japanese research program, *Administrative Science Quarterly*, 30: 198–223.

Mook, D. (1987) *Motivation: The Organization of Action*. New York: Norton.

Morgenson, D. (2004) Democracy's dangers, *Ottawa Citizen*, 9 May: A-12.

Morris, C. (1972) *The Discovery of the Individual: 1050–1200*. London: Camelot.

Mothershead, J.L., Jr (1955) *Ethics: Modern Conceptions of the Principles of Right*. New York: Henry Holt and Company.

Murray, H. (1938) *Explorations in Personality*. New York: Oxford University Press.

Nadler, D. A. and Tushman, M. L. (1990) Beyond the charismatic leader: leadership and organizational change, *California Management Review*, Winter: 77–97.

Neilsen, E. (1986) Empowerment strategies: balancing authority and responsibility, in S. Srivastva et al., *Executive Power: How Executives Influence People and Organizations*. San Francisco: Jossey-Bass.

Novak, M. (1997) John Paul II: Christian philosopher, *America*, 25 October: 12.

Ohmann, O. A. (1989) Skyhooks, in K. R. Andrews (ed.), *Ethics in Practice: Managing the Moral Corporation*, pp. 58–69. Boston: Harvard Business School Press.

Oldham, G. R. (1976) The motivation strategies used by supervisors, *Organizational Behavior and Human Performance*, 15: 66–86.

Organ, D. W. (1988) *Organizational Citizenship Behavior: The Good Soldier Syndrome*. Lexington, MA: Lexington Books.

O'Toole, J. (1985) *Vanguard Management: Redesigning the Corporate Future*. Gorden City, NY: Doubleday.

Ottawa Citizen (2004, March 6). Tracking the scandals, p. D 3.

Ouchi, W. (1981) *Theory Z: How American Business Can Meet the Japanese Challenge*. Reading, MA: Addison-Wesley.

Paine, L. S. (1994) Managing for organizational integrity, *Harvard Business Review*, March–April: 106–17.

Pascale, R. and Athos, A. (1981) *The Art of Japanese Management*. New York: Simon & Schuster.

Peterson, M. F., Maiya, H. and Herreid, C. (1987) *Field Application of Japanese PM Leadership Theory in Two US Service Organizations*. Unpublished manuscript, Texas Technology University, Lubbock, College of Business.

Peterson, M. F., Smith, M. F. and Tayeb, M. H. (1987) *Development and Use of English-Language Versions of Japanese PM Leadership Measures in Electronics Plants*. Proceedings of the annual meeting of the Southern Management Association, New Orleans, November.

Petty, R. E. and Cacioppo, J. T. (1981) *Attitudes and Persuasion: Classic and Contemporary Approaches*. Dubuque, IA: Brown.

Pfeffer, J. (1977) The ambiguity of leadership, *Academy of Management Review*, 2: 104–12.

Pfeffer, J. (1981) Management as symbolic action: the creation and maintenance of organizational paradigms, in L. L. Cumming and B. M. Staw (eds), *Research in Organizational Behavior*, Vol. 3, pp. 1–52. Greenwich, CT: JAI Press.

Pieper, J. (1966) *The Four Cardinal Virtues*. Notre Dame, Indiana: University of Notre Dame Press.

Podsakoff, P. M., Todor, W. D. and Skov, R. (1982) Effect of leader contingent and non-contingent reward and punishment behaviors on subordinate performance and satisfaction, *Academy of Management Journal*, 25: 810–21.

Puffer, S.M. (1999) Global statesman: Mikhail Gorbachev on globalization, *The Academy of Management Executive*, 13 (1): 8–14.

Radhakrishnan, S. (1962) *The Hindu View of Life*. New York: Macmillan.

Rani, M. (1969) *Moral Development in Children*. Unpublished doctoral dissertation, University of Allahabad, India.

Reich, C. (1971) *The Greening of America: How the Youth Revolution is Trying to Make America Livable*. New York: Bantam.

Roberts, N. (1985) Transforming leadership: a process of collective action, *Human Relations*, 38: 1023–46.

Roland, A. (1988) *In Search of Self in India and Japan: Toward a Cross-Cultural Psychology*. Princeton, NJ: Princeton University Press.

Roseman, E. (2002) Most want socially responsible companies, *The Toronto Star*, 1 February, *www.thestar.com*, p. 1.

Rothbaum, F. M., Weisz, J. R. and Snyder, S. S. (1982) Changing the world and changing self: a two process model of perceived control, *Journal of Personality and Social Psychology*, 42: 5–37.

Rotter, J. B. (1966) Generalized expectancies for internal versus external control of reinforcement, *Psychological Monographs*, 80(1): 609.

Rotter, J. and Stein, D. (1971) Public attitudes toward the trustworthiness, competence, and altruism of twenty selected occupations, *Journal of Applied Social Psychology*, 1: 334–43.

Runciman, W. (1978) *Weber in Translation*. Cambridge, MA: Harvard University Press.

Salk, J. (1973) *The Survival of the Wisest*. New York: Harper & Row.

Sampson, E. (1988) The debate on individualism: indigenous psychologies of the individual and their role in personal and societal functioning, *American Psychologist*, 43: 15–22.

Sashkin, M. (1984) Participative management is an ethical imperative, *Organizational Dynamics*, Spring: 5–22.

Sashkin, M. (1988) The visionary leader, in J. A. Conger and R. N. Kanungo (eds), *Charismatic Leadership: The Elusive Factor in Organizational Effectiveness*, pp. 122–60. San Francisco: Jossey-Bass.

Schein, E. H. (1958) The Chinese indoctrination program for prisoners of war: a study of attempted 'brainwashing', in E. E. Maccoby, T. M. Newcomb and E. L. Hartley (eds), *Readings in Social Psychology*, 3rd edn, pp. 311–34. New York: Holt.

Schein, E. H. (1980) *Organizational Psychology*. Englewood Cliffs, NJ: Prentice Hall.

Schein, E. H. (1985) *Organizational Culture and Leadership*. San Francisco: Jossey-Bass.

Schmiesing, K. (2004) *A History of Personalism*. *http://www.acton.org/research/pubs/papers/history_personalism.html*

Schmitz, K.L. (1993) *At the Center of the Human Drama: The Philosophical Anthropology of Karol Wojtyla/Pope John Paul II*. Washington, DC: Catholic University of America Press.

Schwartz, B. (1986) *The Battle for Human Nature*. New York: Norton.

Schwartz, B. (1990) The creation and destruction of value, *American Psychologist*, 45: 7–15.

Schwartz, S. (1975) The justice of need and the activation of humanitarian norms, *Journal of Social Issues*, 31: 111–36.

Second Vatican Council (1963) Pastoral constitution on the Church in the modern world, in W. M. Abbott (ed.), *The Documents of Vatican II*, pp. 199–331. New York: Guild Press.

Second Vatican Council (1965) Declaration on the relationship of the Church to non-Christian religions, in W. M. Abbott (ed.), *The Documents of Vatican II*, pp. 660–8. New York: Guild Press.

Senge, P.M. (1990) *The Fifth Discipline: The Art and Practice of the Learning Organization*. London: UK, Century Business.

Shamir, B., House, R. and Arthur, M. B. (1993) The rhetoric of charismatic leadership: a theoretical extension, a case study, and implications for research, *Leadership Quarterly*, 5(1): 25–42.

Shaw, W. and Barry, V. (1989) *Moral Issues in Business*, 4th edn. Belmont, CA: Wadsworth Publishing Company.

Shepard, J. M. (1971) *Automation and Alienation*. Cambridge, MA: MIT Press.

Siguaw, J.A., Rockness, J.W., Hunt, T.G. and Howe Jr, V. (1998) Ethical values and leadership: a study of AACSB Business School deans, *Proceedings of Academy of Management Conference*, San Diego, California [CD-ROM].

Simon, H. (1990) A mechanism for social selection and successful altruism, *Science*, 250: 1665–8.

Sims, H.P. (1977) The leader as manager of reinforcement contingencies: an empirical example and a model, in J. G. Hunt and L. L. Larson (eds), *Leadership: The Cutting Edge*, pp. 121–37. Carbondale: Southern Illinois University Press.

Sims, H.P. and Lorenzi, P. (1992) *The New Leadership Paradigm*. Newbury Park, CA: Sage.

Singh, P. and Bhandarkar, A. (1990) *Corporate Success and Transformational Leadership*. New Delhi: Wiley Eastern.

Sinha, D. (1972) *The Mughal Syndrome: A Psychological Study of Intergenerational Differences*. New Delhi: Tata-McGraw Hill.

Sinha, J. B. P. (1980) *The Nurturant Task Leader*. New Delhi: Concept.

Sinha, J. B.P. (1990) A model of effective leadership styles in India, in A. M. Jaeger and R. N. Kanungo (eds), *Management in Developing Countries*, pp. 252–63. London: Routledge.

Smart, N. (1983) *Worldviews: Crosscultural Explorations of Human Beliefs*. New York: Scribner.

Smith, A. (1936) *An Inquiry into the Nature and Wealth of Nations*. New York: Modern Library. (Original work published 1776)

Smith, P. B. and Peterson, M. F. (1988) *Leadership, Organizations and Culture*. London: Sage.

Solomon, R.C. (1984) *Morality and the Good Life*. New York: McGraw-Hill.

Spence, J. (1985) Achievement American style: the rewards and costs of individualism. *American Psychologist*, 40: 1285–95.

Spence, J. and Helmreich, R. (1983) Achievement-related motives and behavior, in J. Spence (ed.), *Achievement and Achievement Motives: Psychological Approaches*, pp. 7–74. San Francisco: Freeman.

Spreitzer, G. M. (1995) Individual empowerment in the workplace: dimensions, measurement, validation, *Academy of Management Journal*, 38(5): 1442–65.

Spreitzer, G. M. (1996) Social structural levels for workplace empowerment, *Academy of Management Journal*, 39(2): 483–504.

Srinivas, K.M. (1994) Organization development: Maya or Moksha, in R. N. Kanungo and M. Mendonca (eds), *Work Motivation: Models for Developing Countries*, pp. 248–82. New Delhi: Sage.

Stovall, R. H. (1988) The Trinity Center roundtable – the ethics of corporate leadership, in *Ethics in American Business: A Special Report*, pp. 28–9. New York: Touche Ross.

Strauss, G. (1977) Managerial practices, in J. R. Hackman and L. J. Suttle (eds), *Improving Life at Work: Behavioral Science Approaches to Organizational Change*, pp. 297–363. Santa Monica, CA: Goodyear.

Student, K. R. (1968) Supervisory influence and work-group performance, *Journal of Applied Psychology*, 52: 188–94.

Tannenbaum, R. and Schmidt, W. H. (1958) How to choose a leadership pattern, *Harvard Business Review*, March–April.

Thibaut, J. W. and Kelley, H. H. (1959) *The Social Psychology of Groups*. New York: John Wiley.

Thomas, K. W. and Velthouse, B. A. (1990) Cognitive elements empowerment: an 'interpretive' model of intrinsic task motivation, *Academy of Management Review*, 15: 666–81.

Tichy, N. M. and Devanna, M. A. (1986) *The Transformational Leader*. New York: John Wiley.

Trevino, L. K., Weaver, G. R., Gibson, D. G. and Toffler, B. L. (1999) Managing ethics and legal compliance: what works and what hurts, *California Management Review*, 41 (2): 131–51.

Triandis, H. C. (1984) Toward a psychological theory of economic growth, *International Journal of Psychology*, 19: 79–95.

Triandis, H. C. (1988) Collectivism and development, in D. Sinha and H. S. R. Kao (eds), *Social Values and Development: Asian Perspective*, pp. 285–303. New Delhi: Sage.

Triandis, H. C. (1993) The contingency model in cross-cultural perspective, in N. M. Chemers and R. Ayman (eds), *Leadership Theory and Research*, pp. 167–88. San Diego: Academic Press.

Triandis, H. C. (1994) Cross-cultural industrial and organizational psychology, in H. C. Triandis, M. D. Dunnette and L. M. Hough (eds), *Handbook of Industrial and Organizational Psychology*, 2nd edn, Vol. 4, pp. 103–72. Palo Alto, CA: Consulting Psychologists Press.

Trompenaars, F. (1993) *Riding the Waves of Culture*. London: The Economist Press.

Tuan, Y. (1982) *Segmented Worlds and Self*. Minneapolis: University of Minnesota Press.

Velasquez, M. G. (1982) *Business Ethics*. Englewood Cliffs, NJ: Prentice Hall.

Viega, J. F. and Dechant, K. (1993) Fax poll: altruism in corporate America, *Academy of Management Executive*, 7(3): 89–91.

Virmani, B. R. and Guptam, S. U. (1991) *Indian Management*. New Delhi: Vision.

Vitz, P. C. (1994) *Psychology as Religion: The Cult of Self-Worship*, 2nd edn. Grand Rapids, MI: Eerdmans.

Vroom, V. H. and Yetton, E. W. (1973) *Leadership and Decision Making*. Pittsburgh, PA: University of Pittsburgh Press.

Walster, E., Aronson, D. and Abrahams, D. (1966) On increasing the persuasiveness of a low prestige communicator, *Journal of Experimental Social Psychology*, 2: 325–42.

Walton, C. C. (1988) *The Moral Manager*. Cambridge, MA: Ballinger.

Watson, C. E. (1991) *Managing with Integrity: Insights from America's C.E.Os*. New York: Praeger.

Weaver, G.R., Trevino, L. K. and Cochran, P.L. (1999) Corporate ethics programs as control systems: influences of executive commitment and environmental factors, *The Academy of Management Journal*, 42(1): 41–57.

Weber, M. (1947) *The Theory of Social and Economic Organizations*, trans A.M. Henderson and T. Parsons, ed. T. Parsons. New York: Free Press.

Weber, M. (1958a) *The Protestant Work Ethic and the Spirit of Capitalism*. New York: Academic Press.

Weber, M. (1958b) *The Religions of India: The Sociology of Hinduism and Buddhism*. Glencoe, IL: Free Press.

Weber, M. (1968) *Economy and Society*, Vols 1–3, ed. G. Roth and C. Wittich. New York: Bedminster. (Original work published 1925)

Weigel, G. (2001) *Witness to Hope: The Biography of Pope John Paul II*. New York: Harper Collins.

Westley, F. and Mintzberg, H. (1988) Profiles of strategic vision: Levesque and Iacocca, in J. A. Conger and R. N. Kanungo (eds), *Charismatic Leadership: The Elusive Factor in Organizational Effectiveness*, pp. 161–212. San Francisco: Jossey-Bass.

Whiting, J. W. M. (1960) Resource mediation and learning by identification, in I. Iscoe and H. W. Stevenson (eds), *Personality Development in Children*, pp. 112–26. Austin: University of Texas.

Wilner, A. R. (1984) *The Spellbinders: Charismatic Political Leadership*. New Haven, CT: Yale University Press.

Wilson, E. (1978) *On Human Nature*. Cambridge, MA: Harvard University Press.

Winter, D. (1973) *The Power Motive*. New York: Free Press.

Wojtyla, K. (1979) *The Acting Person*. Dordrecht, Holland: D. Reidel Publishing Company.

Worchel, S., Cooper, J. and Goethals, G. (1988) *Understanding Social Psychology*. Chicago: Dorsey.

Woycke, J. (1990) Managing political modernization: charismatic leadership in the developing countries, in A. M. Jaeger and R. N. Kanungo (eds), *Management in Developing Countries*, pp. 275–86. London: Routledge.

Yukl, G. A. (1998) *Leadership in Organizations*, 4th edn. Upper Saddle River, NJ: Prentice Hall.

Zaleznik, A. (1977) Managers and leaders: are they different? *Harvard Business Review*, May–June: 67–78.

Zaleznik, A. (1990) The leadership gap, *Academy of Management Executive*, 4(1): 7–22.

Zaleznik, A. and Kets de Vries, M. (1975) *Power and the Corporate Mind*. Boston: Houghton Mifflin.

INDEX

156